The Human Sales Factor

ENDORSEMENTS

"We often have little control over the product we sell, or the people to whom we sell it. But Lance Tyson reminds us that we have control over the seller – ourselves. In his concisely entertaining The Human Sales Factor, *we learn how to make ourselves vastly more successful at the essential skills that drive business—our ability to connect and persuade."*

—General Stanley McChrystal, U.S. Army (Retired), *New York Times* Bestselling Author of *Team of Teams*

"This book will absolutely change the way you sell and connect with your clients - not through fake gimmicks to trick people into believing something you don't believe in yourself, but through a curation of the enthusiasm, credibility, and reason you already possess for a product or service you're passionate about! Lance's brilliant writing and stories will keep you learning new skills on every page. Read this book and change the course of your career and company for good!"

— Marshall Goldsmith is the *New York Times* #1 bestselling author of *Triggers, Mojo, and What Got You Here Won't Get You There*

"Success begins with the stories that matter most: the ones we tell ourselves. In this book, Lance Tyson shows how to change the outcome of our stories by leveraging our humanness—our inherent powers of persuasion and influence. This brilliant blueprint for personal and professional success contains riveting anecdotes and eye-opening studies that demonstrate just how powerful our human connections are. If you're looking to increase your odds of persuasion and close the deal, this book is a must read."

—Karen Mangia, Vice President, Salesforce, and Four-Time Author

THE HUMAN

SALES FACTOR

THE H2H EQUATION FOR CONNECTING, PERSUADING AND CLOSING THE DEAL

LANCE TYSON

NEW YORK

LONDON • NASHVILLE • MELBOURNE • VANCOUVER

THE HUMAN SALES FACTOR

The H2H Equation for Connecting, Persuading, and Closing the Deal

This publication is designed to provide accurate and authoritative information in regard to the subject matter covered. It is sold with the understanding that the publisher is not engaged in rendering legal, accounting, or other professional services. If legal advice or other expert assistance is required, the services of a competent professional person should be sought.

Published in New York, New York, by Morgan James Publishing. Morgan James is a trademark of Morgan James, LLC. www.MorganJamesPublishing.com

Proudly distributed by Ingram Publisher Services.

Morgan James BOGO™

A **FREE** ebook edition is available for you or a friend with the purchase of this print book.

CLEARLY SIGN YOUR NAME ABOVE

Instructions to claim your free ebook edition:
1. Visit MorganJamesBOGO.com
2. Sign your name CLEARLY in the space above
3. Complete the form and submit a photo of this entire page
4. You or your friend can download the ebook to your preferred device

ISBN 9781631957055 paperback
ISBN 9781631957062 ebook
ISBN 9781631957918 hardcover
Library of Congress Control Number: 2021943744

Cover Design by:
TGC Worldwide

Interior Design by:
Chris Treccani
www.3dogcreative.net

Morgan James is a proud partner of Habitat for Humanity Peninsula and Greater Williamsburg. Partners in building since 2006.

Get involved today! Visit MorganJamesPublishing.com/giving-back

DEDICATION

To my Lisa, my wife, confidant, coach, and business partner.
Our long talks about dreams, your coaching, and your
encouragement have made all of this possible!

TABLE OF CONTENTS

INTRODUCTION:

Embracing Your Inner Salesperson

• • •

"The greatest ability in business is to get along with others and influence their actions."
-John Hancock

Why does the word "sales" have such a bad rap? Why do people outside the sales industry cringe at the thought of receiving a call or getting an email from a "salesperson"? The answer: in the past, ineffective salespeople have disrupted your world, ripped you away from the million tasks at hand to listen to them try to sell their product or service. Even if it might have been something you wanted or needed, you likely weren't willing to listen because of their approach—pushy, insensitive, self-serving, and/or manipulative.

Part of the reason for this has to do with a concept called *asymmetric information*, which refers to the situation in which a seller has all the product or service knowledge, putting the buyer in a position of vulnerability. And just like with any profession, there are always a few bad actors who make everybody look bad. There are certainly sketchy salespeople out there who use the power of persuasion to manipulate for their own gain, as opposed to creating a *mutual* gain between buyer and seller. But let's not get ahead of ourselves—more on the dark side of influence and persuasion later.

For now, just know that there is one unavoidable fact: *every single one of us is a salesperson.*

Don't believe me? Have you ever pitched someone to believe in your idea? Interviewed for a job? Tried to win a promotion? Have you ever solicited a donation for a charity near and dear to your heart? Tried to convince someone to move a deadline? Have you ever taken a friend out to dinner before you asked for a favor? Do you compliment an acquaintance you hope to do business with? Ever comment on an influencer's social media post hoping they might notice you? Do you dress differently when you want to impress someone? Ever name-dropped to get an edge? How about when you flash a big smile to someone you'd like to know better? Guess what? That's selling.

We're *all* salespeople, just like we're all customers. And if we're all salespeople, that means we all need to understand how things get sold. Ultimately, what makes someone want to do business with someone else? What could you say to make your boss promote you over your colleague? What makes you choose one doctor over another for that elective surgery? What can you do to convince someone to donate to your charity? What makes an investor want to take your idea and run with it? What are the skills and tactics required to *persuade* someone (get them to buy into a new process) or to *influence* them (change their behavior)?

If you've ever watched the show *Shark Tank*, you may have noticed the sharks don't always go for the best idea. When they invest, they invest in the *person*. Therein lies the underpinnings of getting what you want—a secret only the best salespeople, business leaders, entrepreneurs, and thought leaders in the world know: selling, at its core, isn't about moving a product or service, it's about moving *people*. It's about connecting and influencing. You need to understand *how* to connect, how to get into the mind of the person from whom you want something. You must think how they think. You need to understand how they feel. You need to find the mutual benefit that results in getting what you want. Then you need to convince them to act.

> **Selling, at its core, isn't about moving a product or service, it's about moving *people*.**

After spending nearly three decades mastering the skills of connecting and influencing—training and coaching thousands of sales leaders and their teams for some of the biggest brands in the world—I have learned the art of selling and I understand the intricacies of why people buy from others. And despite all the processes, lingo, methodologies, and corporate rhetoric, sales—no matter the industry—has never truly been about selling business-to-business (B2B) or business-to-customer (B2C). Selling always has and always will be done *human-to-human* (H2H).

> **Sales has never truly been about selling business-to-business (B2B) or business-to-customer (B2C). Selling always has and always will be done human-to-human (H2H).**

It all comes down to something I call *The Human Sales Factor*—utilizing the H2H equation for factoring in how people think and process information, adding in the environment and context of the selling situation, multiplied by the person or people who are being persuaded and influenced, and then close the deal. Selling H2H is an individual sport where it's just you against your opponent. And sometimes it's you against *you*. Like a swimmer, wrestler, or golfer, or even a tennis player or decathlon runner, your success is all on *you*. Getting too far into your own head can get in the way.

Even for the most high-performing business leader, salesperson, entrepreneur, solopreneur, social influencer, or soccer parent, the part of the sales process that takes the most time, energy, and resources is making that initial H2H connection. When selling anything, the goal is to create something out of nothing—an opportunity where one did not exist. There are a whole lot of new variables with selling in today's world. Something called COVID-19 changed the rules of the game—maybe not permanently—but for the next decade or so, at least. Virtual conferences, social distancing, limited-capacity sporting events and entertainment venues, online retail, virtual education, video training; new models for our new world are emerging every day.

Maybe you're a C-level executive who wants to master the critical skills of connecting with others and influencing their behaviors. Maybe you're a project manager who wants to become a team leader. Maybe you've stalled out in your career and are looking for some tools to finally get that promotion. Or to land your dream job. Or maybe you're not in the corporate world at all. Maybe you're an up-and-coming entrepreneur or solopreneur looking for investors or industry partners or both. Maybe you're trying to sell your first screenplay to Hollywood. Maybe you're trying to get major donations for your nonprofit. Or maybe you just want to be able to whip out the power of persuasion and get yourself into first class.

Whether you're a seasoned professional or an entrepreneur trying to pitch the next great idea—or maybe you just want to get better at getting what you want—*The Human Sales Factor: The H2H Equation for Connecting, Persuading, and Closing the Deal* is for you. This book is a

> **Persuading and influencing are no longer soft skills.**

peek under the hood of a proven, predictable, scalable process. It's designed for sales leaders and their teams, yet it is still approachable and applicable for the person who just wants to open doors and increase the chances of getting anything they want or need.

Persuading and influencing are no longer soft skills. They are fundamental skills that can help you attract investors, sell products, build brands, inspire teams, and trigger movements. Think about it this way:

- Entrepreneurs influence investors to back their start-ups.
- Job candidates influence recruiters to hire them.
- Politicians persuade people to vote for them.
- Leaders persuade employees to take specific plans of action.
- CEOs influence analysts to write favorable reports about their companies.
- Salespeople persuade customers to choose their product over a competitor's offering.

Selling is 50 percent art, 50 percent science, and 100 percent H2H. The chapters ahead outline the principles, strategies, and tactics needed to succeed. You'll be introduced to the 5 Major Strategies of Emotional Intelligence (EQ). You'll learn about the ancient art of influence and how research and data support social proof as one of the most powerful tools in sales. You'll find real-life examples of H2H selling as well as useful tips to be armed and ready with the H2H skills needed to get what you want when you want it.

Are you ready to embrace your inner salesperson and start opening doors?

CHAPTER ONE:
Selling from the Inside Out

• • •

*"We live in a house of mirrors and think
we are looking out the windows."*
—Frederick Salomon Perls

There once was a guy who lived in a small Midwestern town who was struggling in every aspect of his life. His marriage was suffering. His career was off track. His connections with friends and family were deteriorating.

At his wit's end, he finally confided in one of his childhood friends. "I just don't know how to start getting my life back together. Do you have any advice?"

His friend thought for a minute. "You know that big hill at the west end of town? The one with the house on top?"

The guy shrugged. "Yeah, I've seen it."

"Do you know who lives there?" asked the friend.

"No, who?"

"The Guru. He likes to give advice. Maybe you should see him."

The guy scratched his jaw. "You really think he can help me?"

The friend nodded. "The advice he gave me changed my life. You should go see him."

And that's exactly what the guy did. He walked to the west side of town and scrambled all the way up the hill to the house at the top. Out of breath, he rang the doorbell. Before long, a man with white hair and a face full of wrinkles answered.

"Are you the Guru?" asked the guy.

"I am. Won't you come in," replied the Guru.

The Guru led the man into a sitting room with a large window overlooking the whole town. The guy proceeded to tell the Guru about his struggles with his family, his job, his finances, and his marriage.

"I understand," said the Guru. "Come over to this window for a moment."

The man walked to the window and looked out.

"What do you see?" asked the Guru.

"I see the town."

"What else?"

"I see buildings and houses. I see cars."

"What else?"

The guy leaned closer to the glass. "Well, I see people walking around."

"Who do those people represent?"

"Neighbors. Friends. Family. Clients. Strangers. People I'd like to do business with."

"Good. Now come over here," said the Guru.

The Guru gestured for the guy to stand in front of a great mirror in the corner of the room.

"Now tell me what you see," said the Guru.

"I see myself."

"What is the same about the window and the mirror?"

"They are both glass, of course."

"Right," said the Guru. "And what makes them different."

The guy thought about it a moment. "The mirror has a silver backing on it so I can see my reflection."

The Guru smiled. "Exactly. Therein lies your problem. Once you let a piece of silver get in between you and your field of vision, you will never enjoy success. You need to fix whomever is in the mirror before you can reach whomever is in the window."

This wise Guru understood The Human Sales Factor. H2H selling, at its heart, means first connecting with the human *inside* the mirror before you can connect with any human *outside* the window.

And as the guy in this story finds out, fixing the person in the mirror is a lot more difficult than it sounds. A good friend of mine, Scott McGohan, often says, "Your mind is like a bad neighborhood. You don't want to wander through it alone." That means to effectively execute the powers of persuasion and influence, your first order of business is to clean up the neighborhood.

> H2H selling, at its heart, means first connecting with the human *inside* the mirror before you can connect with any human *outside* the window.

In the pages ahead, you are going to visit the metaphoric mirror to explore and refine your interpersonal skills, attitude control, and communication. If you are ever going to get better at connecting and influencing, you need to deal with your *interiority* first. Only then can you move on to explore your *exteriority*—that is, the window, which represents the strategies, principles, and tactics that can help you achieve your goals.

But before you start looking in the mirror, you need to make sure you understand the nature of persuasion and influence a little better.

Persuasion vs. Influence

Without much reflection, the words *persuasion* and *influence* appear quite similar. But the two concepts are distinct, which require entirely unique skillsets to employ and master. Let's check out what Merriam-Webster has to say:

Persuade

per·suade | \ pər-'swād

1 : to move by argument, entreaty, or expostulation to a belief or position.

- "Monica can persuade audiences to support our cause."

Influence

in·flu·ence | \ 'in-ˌflü-ən(t)s

1 : the power or capacity of causing an effect in indirect or intangible ways.

- "That new boy is a bad influence on Tommy."

Essentially, persuasion moves a person to think differently while influence ignites a behavior. Why does it matter? Well, let's say you are trying to garner a large donation for your favorite charity. One day, a friend invites you to join a foursome for a round of golf. Lo and behold, one of the other golfers happens to be a philanthropic millionaire. Are you going to use persuasion or influence? If you said the latter, you are correct. Because an individual like this is a known philanthropist, she already understands the nature of giving to charity. Being asked for a five- or six-figure donation is nothing new. The key is to use influence to get her to act.

On the other hand, what if this millionaire is a solopreneur who only recently sold her company and made her fortune? She may not understand the concept of making large donations just yet. In this case, persuasion would be the best bet with her—educating her about the concept of philanthropic giving first. If you go asking for a $50,000 donation from someone who has never given such an amount before...well, let's just say it's going to be a long round of golf.

When attempting to persuade and influence others, you really need to understand your own goals, as well as the mindset of person you hope to motivate. You have to ask yourself: Are you selling change? An idea? A concept? Or are you trying to get someone to do something? To invest? To purchase something?

Motivation on both sides of the H2H equation is something you'll cover in greater detail in the next chapter. For now, just know this: To effectively persuade and influence, first you must check your intentions.

The Ethics of Influence

In case you haven't noticed, there has been an endless ebb and flow of self-help books over the decades that continue to dominate our social consciousness and perception when it comes to motivating others so *you* can achieve success. The pages in these books are filled with all sorts of strategies and tactics to influence behavior and persuade thinking. The problem is, most of these books address persuasion and influence superficially. They essentially provide instructions on how to manipulate others using basic interpersonal skills, just so the reader can achieve their goals.

Imagine if the guy in the Guru story simply learned how to smile bigger, how to word his pitch better, how to fake enthusiasm, and how to use his body language to convince others of his sincerity? If you don't master the process of connecting with others and influencing their behavior by looking within yourself first, then success will be fleeting. It's like trying to sail a ship on the ocean without making sure the sails and hull are sound first. Eventually, you're going to sink. And how many others are you going to take with you as a result of your unethical behavior?

Believe it or not, the host of literature out there on achieving your goals through persuasion and influence wasn't always so superficial. Prior to World War II, almost all the literature, stretching back 150 years, focused on a concept called *character ethic*. As Stephen Covey described in his bestseller, *The 7 Habits of Highly Effective People*, "... things like integrity, humility, fidelity, temperance, courage, justice, patience, industry, simplicity, modesty, and the golden rule..." make up the foundation of how enduring success and happiness should be pursued and achieved.[1]

> **If you don't master the process of connecting with others and influencing their behavior by looking within yourself first, then success will be fleeting.**

Somewhere along the lines, however, there was a distinct paradigm shift. Suddenly, the intrinsic motivation and moral principles were replaced by mastering public relation skills and simply having a positive mental attitude. Some of these books, not all, even crossed the line by encouraging readers to be disingenuous

---

1   Covey, Stephen. *The 7 Habits of Highly Effective People*. London: Simon & Schuster, 1999.

and manipulative in order to achieve their goals and get others to like them.

If you use the skills of persuasion and influence insincerely, you might succeed in the short term, but long-term use of this methodology is not sustainable. Someone whose character is fundamentally flawed will never be successful. They will eventually be seen as conniving and deceitful.

Which leads to a potent warning about the content found in this book: Persuasion and influence are dangerous when in the wrong hands.

The Dark Side of Persuasion and Influence

We can all agree that a knife isn't inherently bad. It's a matter of how it's wielded. When you are chopping onions, a knife is a useful tool. But when used to hurt someone else, a knife is deadly. The same can be said for manipulation, which is the tool used in persuasion and influence. It isn't necessarily a bad word. In fact, it means, "to act in a skillful manner." Nothing wrong with that, right? It depends on who uses it, and for what purpose.

In the hands of someone like Adolf Hitler or Charles Manson, the ability to persuade and influence is beyond dangerous. You've likely heard or used the phrase: "drank the Kool-Aid". Let's not forget where that came from. Cult leader, Jim Jones, convinced over 900 of his followers to drink the flavored beverage laced with cyanide, resulting in a mass suicide. And how can we forget Bernie Madoff?

In a lighter example, the powers of persuasion and influence are much like the magic wielded by Slytherin and Gryffindor in the *Harry Potter* series. The character of those in the former house is fundamentally flawed, though their magic is just as potent as that of Harry and company. But who wins in the end?

When used for good, amazing things can be accomplished. Think of Gandhi, Mother Teresa, and Dr. Martin Luther King, Jr., just to name a few who have used the powers of persuasion and influence to make our world a better place. So, you see, persuasion and influence are more than words; they are *powers*. They can make others think and act, for good or for evil.

That's why the mastery of these powerful tools begins in the mirror.

• •

H2H Reflections

- To effectively execute the powers of persuasion and influence, our first order of business is to explore and refine your interpersonal skills, attitude control, and communication.
- Only after you deal with your *interiority* can you move on to explore your *exteriority*.
- *Persuasion* moves a person to think differently while *influence* ignites a behavior. Were you aware of the difference? Have you used these words interchangeably?
- If you use the skills of persuasion and influence insincerely, you might succeed in the short term, but long-term use of this methodology is not sustainable.
- Persuasion and influence are dangerous when in the wrong hands. Use them wisely! Do you know someone who uses their charisma to persuade or influence for less-than-noble intentions? How do you feel about that person?

• •

CHAPTER TWO:

The Greek Mirror

● ● ●

"To live without mirrors is to live without the self."
- Margaret Atwood

Not long ago, I was in Connecticut for a hockey tournament with two of my sons. I was standing out in a parking lot, which was tucked along a wooded edge. As I looked up at the sky, I spotted a bird soaring high overhead. The sun was in my eyes, so I couldn't tell whether it was a vulture or an eagle. Thanks to the miracle of cell phones, I began looking up the differences on the Internet. The article I read said that only a trained eye could see the difference between an eagle and a vulture because the feather coloring is very similar, especially when viewed from the ground. Plus, the wingspan is almost identical.

But there are also some significant differences—like the beak. A vulture has a hooked beak that is designed to dig into an animal that's already dead. An eagle has a beak that is pointed like an arrow-head to pierce and kill. So, think about this: if you had a vulture that was starving and put him in a room with a field mouse, the vulture would eventually die waiting for the mouse to kick the bucket. On the other hand, if a hungry eagle were put in a room with a field mouse, that eagle would hunt down the field mouse with every ounce of energy it had left, or the eagle would die trying.

All of this is to say: the first thing to do when you stand in front of the mirror is look for the eagle. The eagle represents *enthusiasm* in whatever it is you want to achieve. Your enthusiasm is your essence, your being. In fact, enthusiasm is a Greek word that literally means, "God within." Note that the last letters of the word are I-A-S-M. This stands for *I Am Sold Myself.* Before you can ever get someone else to buy into whatever it is you are selling, you must be sold on it first.

> **Before you can ever get someone else to buy into whatever it is you are selling, you must be sold on it first.**

Enthusiasm is not being a cheerleader. It's an underlying intensity. Why is enthusiasm an important element in the Human Sales Factor? Because when sincere, it is one of the most powerful tools in getting someone to buy whatever it is that you are selling. Let me put it this way: if two people are equally matched in skills, education, and experience, the one who is more enthusiastic will win out. Always.

The reason for this has a lot to do with motivation. And even more to do with Maslow.

Motivation and Maslow

Chris Gardner was a salesman…and a single father struggling to make ends meet. When he was evicted from his apartment, he and his young son were suddenly homeless. A chance encounter in a cab eventually led to an unpaid internship at Dean Witter.

But it was a stepping stone for Chris, and his enthusiasm is what got him and his son through the many hardships that followed. In time, Chris became a successful broker and opened his own multimillion-dollar firm. You may recognize Chris' story from the feature film based on his bestselling memoir *The Pursuit of Happyness,* starring Will Smith as Chris Gardner.

Chris' story may have reached the level of notoriety few stories ever reach. But his circumstances aren't totally unique. With the right kind of motivation, *any* dream is possible.

If you look at Maslow's Hierarchy of Needs, Chris was pretty far down on the pyramid.[2]

We're talking about survival mode here. Not just his own survival, but that of his son. Chris had no choice except to succeed.

---

2   "Maslow: Needs Theory." *Motivating to Perform in the Workplace*, 2012, 94-97. doi:10.4324/9780080914602-36.

It's kind of like that old analogy: If two wolves are climbing a hill toward a rabbit, which wolf is going to make it to the top first? The wolf that's the hungriest.

The level of need on Maslow's pyramid often determines the level of enthusiasm. But don't think you literally need to be starving to succeed. Hunger for success, hunger for happiness, hunger for financial freedom, hunger for that promotion, hunger for companionship—these are all valid motivations and equally as powerful as physical hunger.

Once you determine your appetite for success, use your mirror to reflect on the three pillars of influence.

The Three Pillars of Influence

More than 2,000 years ago, the Greek philosopher, Aristotle, detailed a formula on how to master the art of influence in his work, *The "Art" of Rhetoric*.[3] Many great leaders throughout history have employed these techniques to persuade and influence the masses.

To master the art of influence, you need to familiarize yourself with three of Aristotle's five rhetorical devices (the other two devices will be covered later in the book):

1) *Ethos* (Character)

The first thing you ever sell to people is your *ethos*—who you are. This is the origin of the phrase "you never get a second chance to make a first impression". Your buyer, your customer, the gate agent you hope will upgrade you to first class—they are all watch-

---

3   Aristotle, and Freese, John Henry. *The "Art" of Rhetoric*. Cambridge, MA: Harvard Univ. Press, 2000.

ing and judging you. Credibility is made or broken based on your character. Aristotle believed that a person's actions need to back up what they say, or else they lose credibility.

You may have seen a now-famous TED Talk featuring Human Rights Attorney, Bryan Stevenson, on reforming the criminal justice system in which he stated, "I spend most of my time in jails, in prisons, on death row. I spend

> **Humans are hardwired to quickly search for reasons to trust another person.[5]**

most of my time in very low-income communities in the projects and places where there's a great deal of hopelessness."[4] Notice that Stevenson never mentions his degrees or accomplishments. Instead, he establishes his character, which is building his power of influence and persuasion.

Humans are hardwired to quickly search for reasons to trust another person.[5] Think about it—our ancestors only had seconds to determine whether a stranger was a friend or a foe. That's why you smile and shake hands when you first meet someone. You're building trust by making yourself vulnerable and showing you are not armed.

2) *Logos* (Reason)

Once you've established that immediate credibility, you need to make your appeal using logic. Why should the other person

4   Stevenson, Bryan. "We Need to Talk about an Injustice." TED. Accessed October 02, 2021. https://www.ted.com/talks/bryan_stevenson_we_need_to_talk_about_an_injustice?language=en.

5   Freeman. *JNeuro*. PDF file. 2014. http://psych.nyu.edu/freemanlab/pubs/2014Freeman_JNeuro.pdf

care about whatever it is you are selling? If it will save time or money or both, provide evidence. What are the steps they need to take to be successful? How have others benefitted from what you are trying to sell? After all, a smile only goes so far. Use data, evidence, and facts to demonstrate a rational argument.

3) *Pathos* (Emotion)

People evaluate logically but buy emotionally. In fact, Aristotle believed that persuasion isn't possible without emotion. People are moved to action by how the other person makes them *feel.* In sales, this is the heartbeat of the Human Sales Factor. Aristotle argued that the best way to transfer emotion from one person to another is through storytelling. According to an article in *Harvard Business Review*, neuroscientists have proven his theory. These studies have shown that storytelling triggers a rush of neurochemicals in the brain, including oxytocin, which connects people on a deeper, emotional level.[6]

The good news is that even Aristotle agreed that the art of influence can be learned. In fact, according to Professor Edith Hall, the ancient Greek's ideas were considered "quite threatening" to the political class because these tools were made available to the masses.[7] The elitists wanted to keep this formula a closely guarded secret. Had that been successful, it's unlikely that you would have ever had access to these critical underpinnings of the Human Sales Factor.

---

6   "Why Your Brain Loves Good Storytelling." Harvard Business Review. November 05, 2014. Accessed October 02, 2021. https://hbr.org/2014/10/why-your-brain-loves-good-storytelling.

7   Hall, Edith. *Aristotle's Way: How Ancient Wisdom Can Change Your Life.* London: Penguin, 2019.

The ability to influence, to persuade hearts and minds, is perhaps the greatest skill that exists. Mastering this skill will give you a competitive edge in all you do, both personally and professionally. Some economists even claim that persuasion and influence are so powerful they are responsible for generating one-quarter or more of America's total national income.[8]

Some economists even claim that persuasion and influence are so powerful they are responsible for generating one-quarter or more of America's total national income.

But mastering the art of persuasion to be able to close the deal takes more than just practice. It takes a little something called Emotional Intelligence, colloquially known as EQ.

. . . .

H2H Reflections

- The first thing you need to do when you stand in front of the mirror is look for the eagle. The eagle represents *enthusiasm* in whatever it is you want to achieve. Have you been more like an eagle or a vulture?
- If two people are equally matched in skills, education, and experience, the one who is more enthusiastic will always win out.
- Where do you currently find yourself on Maslow's Hierarchy of Needs? Where do you find the person or people you hope to influence or persuade?
- The first thing you ever sell to people is your *ethos*—who you are.

---

8   McCloskey, Deidre. "How to Buy, Sell, Make, Manage, Produce, Transact, Consume with Words" PDF file. June 28, 2007. https://www.deirdremccloskey. com/docs/words.pdf

- Use *logos*—data, evidence, and facts—to demonstrate a rational argument.
- Sharpen up your *pathos* skills—people evaluate logically but buy emotionally.

• •

CHAPTER THREE:

H2H = EQ⁵

• • •

"Setting an example is not the main means of influencing others.
It is the only means."
- Albert Einstein

For many, collecting watches is a guilty pleasure. A watch signifies so many things—time, commitment, longevity, patience, perseverance. Time is what you struggle to keep with those you love and win with those whom you hope to connect or do business. Time is a crucial component in the H2H equation because you are asking someone to give it away, banking on the fact that there's going to be a mutual ROI.

Kate understands this concept of time very well. When buying watches, she's the salesperson I typically do business with. In late February of 2020, she sent me a nice note: "I'm still looking for that Omega watch you were interested in." Three weeks later, COVID-19 broke out in the US and everything went into lockdown. I had barely made a dent in my stockpile of toilet paper and hand sanitizer when Kate reached out again via text: "Hey Lance, I know this text message is probably not appropriate, however, I did find that Omega watch. I know you're not going to buy it now, but when things change—and I know they will—I do have it for you. I hope all is well and your family is safe and healthy."

> Too many times I watch salespeople try to sell with only one gear—maximum overdrive. They just don't have the tactical empathy required to succeed.

Was Kate selling during an extremely sensitive, difficult time? Absolutely. Was it appropriate? Some of you reading this might not think so. But between knowing what she knew of me, and more importantly, the tone she used, I would say that was probably the right strategy. She was planting seeds for the future. She got into my head and anticipated the things I might be thinking. Too many times I watch salespeople try to sell with only one gear—maximum overdrive. They just don't have the tactical empathy required to succeed.

When you think about it, buyers come from all sorts of backgrounds, have all kinds of different experiences, and might have a lot more information than you—or a different version of information. You've got to somehow get into their heads and enable them to share, so you can help them ultimately weigh out the best decision. But what is the key to unlocking the door to a buyer's mind?

It's a secret weapon called *EQ*.

The Lowdown on EQ

Your Emotional Quotient (EQ), the psychological equivalent of your Intelligence Quotient (IQ), is "the capacity for recognizing our own feelings and those of others, for motivating ourselves, and for managing emotions well in ourselves and in our relationships."[9] EQ is an absolute requirement for effective and sustainable relationships. Like persuasion and influence, EQ should never be regarded as a soft skill in business. EQ is critical to both personal *and* professional success.

I wrote a short bestseller in 2020 on the subject called *Igniting Sales EQ*, which essentially is a guide for salespeople to learn how to control their attitude, leverage interpersonal skills, and rely on strong communication skills to connect with buyers. Because all sales involve the Human Sales Factor, the high-EQ person realizes that they are dealing with different factors in the sales process that cause stress, uncertainty, and change. And who's the only person in the whole world you can change? That's right. *You*! Do you find it easy or hard to change yourself? It's hard. It's so hard, in fact, that we spend most of our time trying to change everybody else.

The key to igniting your sales EQ is understanding that people will size you up and draw their conclusions about you based on what they see and how you act. How you display yourself to the world will determine their impression of you. Or if they want to do business with you. The most successful entrepreneurs and business leaders exhibit behavioral activity that matches

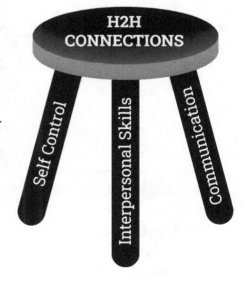

9   Daniel Goleman, *Working with Emotional Intelligence* (New York: Bantam Books, 1998).

those who they are dealing with, those who go out of their way to make that H2H connection.

But EQ isn't just one dimension nor one aspect of your personality. It's so much more than being nice, opening the door for others, or remembering someone's birthday. I like to think of EQ as a three-legged stool upon which H2H connections are built.

The first of the three legs in the stool is the oh-so-difficult *self-control*.

Self-Control

Controlling your actions and words requires a good helping of self-awareness—the ability to recognize an emotion as it happens. Developing self-awareness requires facing your true feelings. If you take time to think through your emotions, you can manage them…and understand their effects on others.

The thing is, most people rate their own EQ as high, yet only a fraction of those individuals are rated as emotionally intelligent by others. Turning this kind of self-deception into self-awareness won't happen without feedback, the kind that comes from data-based assessments such as valid personality tests or 360-degree feedback surveys. These tools are fundamental in helping you uncover EQ-related blind spots, mostly because other people are generally too polite to give you constructive feedback.

> **Most people rate their own EQ as high, yet only a fraction of those individuals are rated as emotionally intelligent by others.**

The person you want to sell to may be human, but so are you. It's okay to *have* emotions. Negative feelings like anger, anxiety, or depression are normal. But you need to monitor how you express them. For example, if you wake up to a bunch of annoying emails, don't respond immediately. Wait until you have time to calm down. Likewise, if someone makes an irritating comment during a meeting, control your reaction, and keep calm. While you can't exactly go from being Darth Vader to the Dalai Lama overnight, you can avoid stressful situations and inhibit your volatile reactions by being aware of your triggers.

One way to raise your EQ is to recast a frustrating situation in a more positive light by taking a long walk or spending a few minutes in meditation or prayer.

Interpersonal Skills

Hopefully by this stage in life you have some grasp on the concept of empathy. An empathetic person excels at sensing what others' needs are and what they might be feeling based on certain situations. In the opening anecdote of this chapter, Kate showed tremendous empathy in sensing my hesitation to buy a watch after the lockdowns happened. Those kinds of interpersonal skills that are critical to making and maintaining H2H connections.

Selling can be very complex. That means there may be a lot of personalities to read and juggle. To succeed, you need to have a high EQ to better understand and negotiate with others in a global economy. Outside of empathy, other interpersonal skills required to build those H2H connections include being open-minded, becoming proficient in resolving disagreements, knowing how to nurture relationships, collaborating, cooperating, and getting in sync with your team to work toward common goals.

Communication

Communication means so much more than talking. It means listening to understand, not just to respond. It means paying attention to the tone of someone's voice and their body language.

This is especially important in the virtual realm. The better you are at understanding the feelings behind others' verbal and body language, the better you can control the signals you send them.

> **Communication means so much more than talking. It means listening to understand, not just to respond.**

Good communication also means sounding interested in the conversation, making a connection with others, and being able to persuade people. This is where you can stand out as an influencer, send clear messages, and inspire others to take action.... like getting that upgrade to first class.

Raising your EQ to be able to influence and persuade in our complex world is a purposeful effort. Because it can be such a difficult task, you also need to develop something else. Grit.

Got Grit?

Mike Ondrejko is the President of Global Sales for Legends˚, a premium experiences company that specializes in delivering unique and custom solutions in naming rights, sponsorship, premium ticket sales, fundraising, conferences, events, and tours for iconic facilities including SoFi Stadium, the University of Notre Dame, Las Vegas Raiders, The Ohio State University, Columbus Crew SC, One World Observatory, and the Rose Bowl. Since 2013, Mike has led the Global Sales team to secure over $1 billion in strategic partnership deals and premium ticket sales revenue.

Pretty impressive, right? Well, don't think getting to this level of sales success came easily. Nothing worth doing ever does. Mike got to where he is today because of what all high-EQ salespeople have—what Angela Duckworth calls "Grit" in her book *Grit: The Power of Passion and Perseverance*.

Early in his career, Mike was offered a position as the Senior Vice President of Corporate Hospitality for Madison Square Garden Entertainment Corp. (MSG Entertainment). MSG Entertainment is "the world's most famous arena", so for someone in sports and entertainment like Mike, opportunities don't get much bigger. Mike had to go from zero to sixty—from the mom-and-pop set-up of a traditional sports team to a large, publicly-traded, matrixed organization, where the sports team itself is just one of many priorities. On top of that, they were about to embark on a billion-dollar renovation project.

Now to put this in context, up to that point in time, MSG Entertainment wasn't used to needing to sell anything. For them, bringing in clients was like flipping a light switch. But Mike wanted to introduce some new products and services that related to the renovation, which were going to take some serious selling.

Mind you, he was used to having one conversation, watching the head nod, then going off into the sunset with his idea. Now he had to be smart enough to figure out how to communicate an idea across several different divisions, several different layers of leadership, to get everybody to buy in. Needless to say, he had no playbook. What he wanted to do had never been done. So, what did he do? He asked a lot of questions. He found internal advocates and coaches to use as sounding boards: "How does this work? Why is this happening in this way? I need to figure out how this operates."

He also knew he needed to shield his team from all the layers of management within MSG Entertainment, so they didn't get discouraged. He wanted them to have all the encouragement, tools, coaching and guidance they needed to go out and execute, with no distractions. He built an awesome sales team at MSG Entertainment from the ground up, armed with a powerful combination of skill and attitude. Mike's grit would come into play when, unexpectedly, the billion-dollar Madison Square Garden renovation project was delayed. Not a couple of days or a couple of weeks. The delay was an entire *year*.

That meant all the sales reps who busted their butts to get commitments weren't going to get those big commissions just yet. It meant that all the brands who already committed were now going to be told to wait, with Mike and his team praying those brands didn't get turned off and walk away.

Mike had to harness some serious grit, not to mention his high EQ, to ride out this storm. He knew his number one priority was to protect his sales team. "Yeah, this sucks," he told them. "But now our job is to make sure that we're in position to tell our clients and our partners exactly what's happening. We need to be transparent, truthful, and confident."

As for his clients, he knew he needed to look at the long game. Based on the contractual language, he could certainly squeeze a couple more pennies out of them for the year. But he knew if he treated them fairly and focused on the long-term relationship, it would eventually pay off. At least he hoped it would. A year later, the renovation project was back up and running, construction was happening everywhere, and the clients-in-waiting were excited to get things rolling.

And then the financial meltdown of the late 2000s hit.

It was a one-two punch to Mike and his sales team because many of the clients happened to be financial institutions that relied on Troubled Asset Relief Program (TARP) funds to survive. This meant they couldn't spend taxpayer money on internal services that could be seen as "excessive." Many sales leaders would have thrown in the towel by then. But not Mike Ondrejko. He knew, as the saying goes, that tough times don't last; tough people do.

He needed to redefine what success meant. Instead of the black and white world where anything less than a sale was considered a failure, now success was to be found in every lead. Every call taken. Every meeting set. Every advancement of a relationship. And guess what happened?

The very day the TARP funds were paid back by the financial institutions, his phone rang. And rang. And rang. All the clients came running back. They now had money, and they wanted to spend it with a partner they trusted who respected their position.

Mike looks back on that scenario and says it was the best learning environment that he's ever experienced. He went on to secure over $450 million in suite commitments to help fund the ongoing transformation of MSG Entertainment, in addition to developing sales and marking strategies to engage C-level leaders.

You can coach all day long for skills, and you can always pick up knowledge. But the piece Mike has, that attitude and grit, is something crucial that must be pulled from deep inside oneself.

Raising your EQ to leverage H2H interactions and the ability to connect, persuade, and close deals in a complex world takes dedication. You must have that common denominator of results-driven grit for success. You must persevere. The sales profession is difficult. You get your butt kicked on a daily basis. People say no to you nine times out of ten. People lie to you and act like your friend, then dodge your calls. If you don't have true sales grit like Mike Ondrejko, at the end of the day, you're going to get your butt kicked, too.

But like I said before, selling is 50 percent science. So, let's dive into the science and look at an EQ equation that will boost your abilities to persuade and influence.

Five Strategies of EQ

Now that you understand the fundamentals of EQ, let's talk strategy. There are 5 Major Strategies to EQ, and each of which must be understood, embraced, and put into practice before you even think of mastering the Human Sales Factor. Let's take them from the top:

Negative self-talk can cause your behavior to reflect what you expect to happen rather than what you want to happen.

1. Maintaining a Positive Mindset

A person's mindset has a major impact on how you will interact with other people. Your mindset is strongly impacted by one's self-talk. Self-talk is your internal dialogue, which reveals a person's thoughts and questions. Negative self-talk can cause your behavior to reflect what you expect to happen rather than what you want to happen. Keep in mind:

- Positive self-talk leads to a positive outcome
- Negative self-talk leads to a negative outcome

2. Turning Self-Deception into Self-Awareness

Personality, and thereby EQ, is composed of two parts: 1) identity, or how we see ourselves, and 2) reputation or how others see us. For most people, there is a disparity between identity and reputation that can cause them to ignore feedback and derail their efforts. Real self-awareness is about achieving a realistic view of one's strengths and weaknesses.

3. Turning Self-Focus into Other-Focus

Paying due attention to others is tantamount to career success. But for those with lower levels of EQ, it's difficult for them to see things from other perspectives, especially when there isn't clear right or wrong path forward. Developing an other-centric approach starts with a basic appreciation and acknowledgement of team members' individual strengths, weaknesses, and beliefs. Brief but frequent discussions with team members will lead to a more thorough understanding of how to persuade and influence others. Such conversations should inspire ways to create opportunities for collaboration, teamwork, and external networking.

> Developing an other-centric approach starts with a basic appreciation and acknowledgement of team members' individual strengths, weaknesses, and beliefs.

4. Becoming More Rewarding to Deal With

People who are more employable and successful in their career tend to be seen as more rewarding to deal with. These people tend to be cooperative, friendly, trusting, and unselfish. People who aren't very rewarding to deal with, on the other hand, tend to be more guarded and critical. They are willing to speak their minds and disagree openly but can develop a reputation for being argumentative, pessimistic, and confrontational.

5. Controlling Temper Tantrums

Seriously, you're not three years old anymore. Passion and intense enthusiasm can easily cross the line to become moodiness and outright excitability when the pressure is on. Nobody likes a crybaby. In the business world, those who become particularly disappointed or discouraged when unanticipated issues arise are viewed as undeserving of a seat at the grown-ups' table. If you're one of many people who suffer from too much emotional transparency, reflect on which situations tend to trigger feelings of anger or frustration. Monitor your tendency to overreact in the face of setbacks.

> **We live in a world that rewards people for hiding their insecurities, but the truth is that it is much more important to hide one's arrogance.**

H2H selling takes mental toughness and confidence, but the most-effective people are the ones who come across as humble. Striking a healthy balance between assertiveness and modesty, demonstrating receptiveness to feedback, and admitting one's mistakes, are some of the most difficult tasks to master. We live in a world that rewards people for hiding their insecurities, but the truth is that it is much more important to hide one's arrogance. hat means swallowing one's pride, picking and choosing battles, and looking for opportunities to recognize others even if you feel you are right and others are wrong.

When you begin to see the Human Sales Factor as simply connecting with another human being, all filtered through the lens of EQ, you *will* reach your goals to persuade and influence. The thing is, we have no choice but to become experts at creating rapport and connecting with people. In a rapidly changing marketplace, we need the best odds to be able to do that. People sell to people, and people buy from people. It may sound obvious, but the human being we shake hands with when we strike a deal, virtually or in person, must be someone we connect with on an emotional level. Those first interactions are the foundation for making that emotional connection.

And in the end, all you are trying to do is get the other person to say *yes* over and over again. It's an algorithm of questions, each followed by five or six yeses:

- "Yes, I'll talk to you."
- "Yes, you can ask me questions."
- "Yes, you can present me an idea."
- "Yes, you resolved my objection."
- "Yes, I'll buy."

Sometimes it's challenging to get those yeses. But there's a simple solution—replicable strategy that incorporates the tactics needed to win valuable time on people's calendars and open doors that were previously closed. It's exactly what you need to connect, persuade, and close the deal. It combines creativity with a proven process for predictable results to get those meetings and those yeses.

If EQ is the heartbeat of the Human Sales Factor, then this is the blood: The Read-Offense Mindset. This is something that can be applied to any market condition, across any industry, with any landscape.

. . . .

H2H Reflections

- Raising your EQ by balancing Attitude Control, Interpersonal Skills, and Communication will go a long way in fostering H2H connections. So will digging deep to find the grit and endurance needed to succeed in sales.

- Be sure to memorize and master the equation H2H=EQ^5, which is comprised of The 5 Major Strategies for EQ success:
  - Maintaining a Positive Mindset
  - Turning Self-Deception into Self-Awareness
  - Turning Self-Focus into Other-Focus
  - Becoming More Rewarding to Deal With
  - Controlling Temper Tantrums
- Which of the 5 Major Strategies is your strongest skill? Which one is your weakest?

• •

CHAPTER FOUR:
The Read-Offense Mindset

• • •

*"It is not the strongest of the species that survives,
nor the most intelligent;
it is the one most adaptable to change."*
— Charles Darwin

Picture this: you're a Super Bowl winning quarterback, let's say, Tom Brady. You walk out of the huddle with a play called. But when you get to the line of scrimmage, you see the defense is in a completely unexpected formation. If you want to score, you're going to opt for a Read-Offense strategy—looking at how the other team is positioned and adapt to the situation in the moment.

Or imagine Kobe Bryant walking up and setting up the offense for a half-court press, then seeing the other team do something unexpected. He was certainly going to adapt to the situation. In hockey, a power play always occurs unexpectedly and the opportunity to score happens in the moment.

Leaving the sports metaphors behind, let's say you need to have a stent put into your heart. The surgeon who is going to perform the operation goes into it with a certain plan in mind. But what happens if your blood pressure suddenly drops? Well, in the moment, that doctor is going to have to make some decisions. This might be a very standard surgery, but the blood pressure drop means other decisions need to be made—fast. Or look at the Navy SEALs, where they practice several strategies for any given operation because they never know when things might go sideways.

Read-Offense. This is the new mindset that aligns with the Human Sales Factor. If you want to be able to sell anything to anyone at any time, you need to take a lesson from Charles Darwin, the British naturalist and biologist. Most people get his quote on survival all wrong. It's not "survival of the fittest" or "only the strong survive." That's what we were all improperly taught. What Darwin actually said about the likelihood of a species surviving was this: "It is not the strongest of the species that survives, nor the most intelligent; it is the one most adaptable to change."[10]

And if you don't believe Charles Darwin, then check out the data:

Florida State University (FSU) did a study in 2012 of high-performing salespeople.[11] The study was performed in part to contest the Challenger Sales model, and it was commissioned in response to the influx of questions to the FSU Sales Institute by hundreds of sales executives all wanting to know the same thing: which sales methodology is best for their company?

---

10   Darwin, Charles. *The Origin of Species*. New York: Boston, 1925.
11   Florida State University, Sales Institute. *Why 'Agile' Salespeople Outperform Challengers*. PDF file. 2012. https://ww1.prweb.com/prfiles/2019/04/11/16238761/why-agile-outperforms-challenger.pdf

Researchers went on to survey 783 salespeople from eight different industries to self-identify their individual sales style.[12] At first, the results pretty much validated the body of research done earlier: high performers identified themselves as challenger or consultative sellers while low performers identified as product or relational sellers.

But then, one brave high performer spoke his truth. "I can't fill out your survey," he told researchers, "as the kind of seller I am depends on the selling situation I'm in." His statement got the attention of the researchers. A single sales strategy couldn't work for every sales scenario. Now they needed to dig into the minds of other high performers to see if the same was true for them. Did they shift strategies based on the situation they were in?

This new study targeted 1,500 salespeople from three different industries to explain the various situations they faced and how they sold in each situation. The results? Let's just say, *it depends*, was the common theme among all 1,500 high-performers. The top 10 to 15 percent of sellers had three to four different selling strategies, altering their approach depending on the selling situation. Lower performers generally used just one or two strategies.

> **Companies that forced their sales teams to adopt and use a single strategy ended up churning out average and below-average sales metrics.**

The research also revealed something else. Companies that forced their sales teams to adopt and use a single strategy ended up churning out average and below-average sales metrics.

---

12   Florida State University, Sales Institute. *Why 'Agile' Salespeople Outperform Challengers*. PDF file. 2012.

Improving your chances of making that connection and influencing someone else to act means you must be adaptable, be agile, and be pliable. Recently, one of our Business Development Directors, Brandon Lawrence, was able to get an appointment with Rock Central, which is in the family of companies owned by billionaire business mogul, Dan Gilbert. Brandon previously worked for the Cleveland Cavaliers, which is owned by Dan Gilbert. With that experience, Brandon had inside knowledge that Dan Gilbert has several -isms he lives by, one being a standing rule to always reply to emails within 24 hours.

So, Brandon emailed Dan and said,

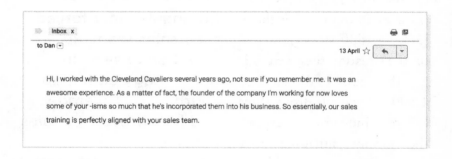

Dan's assistant got back to Brandon right away. "Brandon, here are the people you need to talk to." She copied a few individuals, indicating that Dan was going to meet with Brandon.

Brandon had done his homework in his pre-approach. Then he nailed down an indirect referral from Dan Gilbert himself and Dan's assistant. Of course, he researched the other individuals copied on the email. Those three additional people were, after all, potential influencers, or buyers.

Brandon was well aware that he was approaching someone who was at a higher corporate level than himself, so he knew Dan had a lot of leverage. Brandon also knew he needed to separate himself from the competition and move that meeting to a next step. If during that next meeting, Dan's people came out of the gate and said that they were happy with their current situation, how should Brandon have responded? What if they came out of the gate and asked Brandon to send them some information to review? What if they fully engaged him?

Brandon needed to be prepared to adjust on the fly, no matter what scenario

> **You need to be able to pivot if you want to persuade, and that means you need a Read-Offense Mindset.**

unfolded. Just like how air traffic control needs to be prepared for a storm. Just like a quarterback who may need to call an audible and change the play at the line of scrimmage. Just like a surgeon needs to have a plan B, C, D, and E ready to go when plan A doesn't work. When trying to influence behavior, be ready to handle the unexpected. You need to be able to pivot if you want to persuade, and that means you need a Read-Offense Mindset. Having a Read-Offense Mindset will prepare you for the challenges and uncertainty so you can handle any H2H situation with confidence.

Even Black Swan events.

Navigating Black Swan Events

If you're unfamiliar with the term, a Black Swan event simply means an event that is both unpredictable and devastating. More than an earthquake or tornado that affects a region, a Black Swan's impact is extremely widespread, typically global.

Though each Black Swan is unique and unable to be forecast by even the wisest and most well-equipped leaders, they do occur with some frequency. The oil crisis of the 1970s. The Gulf

War. The Dot-Com crash of the late 1990s. The terrorist attacks on September 11, 2001. The housing market collapse in the late 2000s. COVID-19.

The fact is, there are always going to be conditions that drive markets to switch, products to become more or less popular, that influence the way people buy. Think of how the market changed from purchasing CDs and full albums to how it's done now: releasing and streaming and downloading individual songs.

Change happens. It's our job to roll with it.

Look at the impact streaming services have had on the film and television industry.

From economic disasters to war to social shifts to technological breakthroughs, the markets are always changing, no matter the industry you are in. As a business leader or entrepreneur—or just another human trying to get that raise or that extra 10 percent off on a big screen TV from last week's sale—your job is not to fight the changes in the market. Your job is to interpret the market and figure out how to sell your product or service.

Don't get caught up in the hype and panic. The economy will change just as it always has. Buyers' priorities will change, just as they always have. And competition for budgets and spending will become more fierce, just like they always have. Change happens. It's our job to roll with it.

There was a book published a few years ago called *Blue Ocean Strategy*.[13] The theory presented was that a blue ocean indicates that the water is deep, has a lot of fish, and has fewer people

---

13   Kim, W. Chan, and Mauborgn, Renée. *Blue Ocean Strategy: How to Create Uncontested Market Space and Make the Competition Irrelevant.* Harvard Business Review Press, 2015.

fishing. Black Swan events mean many businesses suddenly find themselves in a red ocean; shallow water, fewer fish, more competitive fishing, bloody with competition.

But the fact is, everybody wants or needs *something*. That will never change, no matter the environment. The key is to select the right strategy. Do you understand your buyer enough to apply the Human Sales Factor? Do you have the right mindset (Read-Offense) and the skillset (EQ) to play the persuasion and influence game?

But the real question is: Do you even know the rules of the game?

• •

H2H Reflections

- If you want to be able to sell anything to anyone at any time, you need to be adaptable to change.
- Having a Read-Offense Mindset will prepare you for the challenges and uncertainty so you can handle any H2H situation with confidence.
- How do you handle Black Swan events?
- Have you ever approached someone with a pitch for something in mind, but based on their reaction had to pivot quickly? Were you successful? Did you feel stumped?

• •

CHAPTER FIVE:

The Rules of Persuasion and Influence

• • •

"Persuasion is often more effectual than force."
—Aesop

Pick a team sport—basketball, hockey, football, soccer—you name it. When you distill all strategies to their simplest forms, the game comes down to players doing one of two things: 1) score, or 2) set up to score. That's it. And when it comes to selling H2H, your job exists for one of two reasons: 1) to persuade or influence someone in the moment,

> When it comes to selling H2H, your job exists for one of two reasons: 1) to persuade or influence someone in the moment, or 2) to connect so you can later compel someone to think or behave differently.

or 2) to connect so you can later compel someone to think or behave differently.

Creating opportunities to persuade or influence when you're looking to get a new job, or land a meeting with a venture capitalist, or get a producer to read your script is easier said than done. Forty-two percent of salespeople say that making that initial connection is the most challenging part of the sales process.[14] Yet, the fact is, connecting is a necessary evil...for both the buyer *and* the seller. HubSpot Research found that 72 percent of companies with fewer than fifty new opportunities per month generated by their sales teams didn't come close to helping the company achieve their revenue goals.[15] Compare that to just 15 percent of companies with 51 to 100 new opportunities generated per month through new connections. Remember, connecting is the first step in the Human Sales Factor, and if done properly, it will eventually lead to a win-win for the buyer and the seller—a solution presented in the sale.

Back in the day, a "win" was often determined by the number of meetings at Starbucks you made each week. Or maybe the number of producers you convinced to read your script. But with all the changes in the market, you need to completely rethink what defines a "win." Right now, just getting someone to respond to an email should be considered a win. The days of taking those small victories for granted are gone, at least for the next few years.

In this new business reality, a "win" is much more incremental. It's not the homerun, the touchdown, the goal of yesterday; it's the

---

14   Gerencer, Tom. "200 Sales Statistics [Cold Calling, Follow-up, Closing Rates]." Zety. May 28, 2021. Accessed October 02, 2021. https://zety.com/blog/sales-statistics.

15   Gerencer, Tom. "200 Sales Statistics [Cold Calling, Follow-up, Closing Rates]." Zety. May 28, 2021.

short strides and getting on base—the simplest of things, such as confirming or updating information or data. Every yard gained is a victory. It's getting a new name of someone to call, or an email address when there was only a phone number previously. The instant gratification of the past is no more.

> **In this new business reality, a "win" is much more incremental. It's not the homerun, the touchdown, the goal of yesterday; it's the short strides and getting on base—the simplest of things, such as confirming or updating information or data.**

Remember playing Chutes & Ladders® when you were a kid? For the uninitiated, this board game is a race against other players to reach the top while avoiding slides and climbing ladders. Right now, the landscape of selling means that you may be going down chutes and have to move with agility to get up a ladder. So, a move might not always progress upward; it may regress downward. Then you'll have to re-establish your position to move upward.

Now that you've redefined what a win is, it's time to understand the rules of the persuasion and influence game. After all, how can you win if you don't know how to play?

Rule #1: Always Maintain Good Balance

No matter what is being sold or to whom, there are two levels of competition—direct and indirect. Direct competitors are competing to persuade the same person with a similar product or service. In addition, there is also anyone and everyone else begging for time, from business service providers and office supplier to HR consultants and IT services. Or let's say you are hoping to get last minute reservations at a popular restaurant on a Saturday night.

You know the place is booked and the manager is overwhelmed—not only with people like you asking to make an exception—but they are also constantly preoccupied with staffing issues, inventory, and all the other demands of their role.

So how do you stand out from the competition? How do you get noticed above all the noise? By having good *balance*. Just like a hockey player needs a strong sense of balance to stay on his skates, selling H2H requires you to develop and practice balance as well. You need to know how to effectively balance these three things:

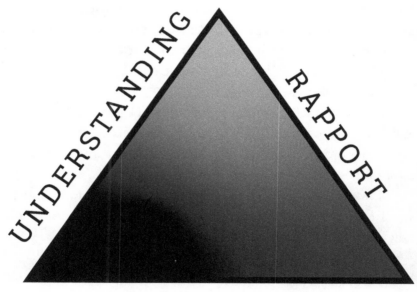

Based on industry knowledge and years of selling both traditionally and virtually, I've found that maintaining this balance while reaching out to the target will increase the odds of being successful and standing out. Here are a few questions you need to consider:

- How will you demonstrate that you *understand* the person you are trying to persuade or influence?
- How will you position yourself as *credible*?
- How will you use human relations to build stronger *rapport*?

Successful people prepare responses to these questions before reaching out to a perspective buyer in order to better appeal to them. Rapport yields influence, which ultimately drives a change in behavior. Can you build a connection enough that someone recognizes you? Credibility yields trust, which ultimately puts you on the path to persuasion. Do you do what you say you'll do when you say you'll do it? Do you follow through?

To stand out to that restaurant manager to persuade her to squeeze you in on a busy Saturday night, perhaps start with defining your loyalty to build rapport. "This is one of my favorite restaurants in town. You may have noticed my name on the reservation list over the years…" Here, a long history of patronage was established—a satisfied customer who has spent a lot of money at the restaurant. "I know you must be incredibly busy with it being a Saturday night and all…" Here an understanding for the man-

> **Rapport yields influence, which ultimately drives a change in behavior. Can you build a connection enough that someone recognizes you? Credibility yields trust, which ultimately puts you on the path to persuasion. Do you do what you say you'll do when you say you'll do it?**

ager's position is being shown. "It would really mean a lot if you could squeeze me and a guest in sometime tonight…." And away you go with the ask. Here's the thing: the manager will either say yes or no. No means disappointing a loyal customer. It means risking future business. It means that some other manager in some other restaurant that Saturday night will accommodate and earn your business. What do you think the manager might say?

Alternatively, if you *always* keep the Human Sales Factor in mind, you might have had the foresight to introduce yourself to the manager on an earlier visit. People are much easier to persuade when you have that rapport, understanding, and credibility already built and balanced.

Rule # 2: Selling is Not About Relationships

Would you like to know what the best sales book of all time is? If you said this one, you're close. The book I'm talking about was written by the great American artist and poet, Theodor Geisel— more familiarly known as the beloved Dr. Seuss. The book: *Green Eggs and Ham.*[16]

Before you think I've lost my mind for calling *Green Eggs and Ham* the best sales book ever written, consider this. Sam-I-Am rejected the offer to eat green eggs and ham *seventy-three times* before he finally relented. Seventy-three rejections! What was the objection the green-egg pusher dealt with seventy-three times? If you did your homework, the objection was simply, "I do not like green eggs and ham."

The next question I have for you is: What was the *first* objection? Ahh, there's the trick! It's not, "I do not like green eggs and

---

16 "Green Eggs and Ham by Dr. Seuss." Goodreads. January 01, 1988. Accessed October 05, 2021. https://www.goodreads.com/book/show/23772.Green_Eggs_and_Ham.

ham." The first objection in the book is: "I do not like that Sam-I-Am." So, the first objection in the book was to the actual *human*.

Sometimes the objection of the person is because that person did something the buyer didn't like. Sometimes that objection is an act of omission. Maybe it's not what you said or did, but what you *didn't* say or do. Maybe the potential buyer didn't like your shirt or how you carried yourself. Sales is *not* about relationships. The word *relationship* is one of the most overused frameworks in business and sales.

> **Sales is *not* about relationships.**

Now, I completely agree with Mark McCormick who wrote in his book, *What They Don't Teach You at Harvard Business School*, "If all things were equal, people would buy from people they liked. If all things weren't so equal, they'd still buy from people they liked."[17] I'm not arguing that there is a likeability factor in selling. In fact, that was Sam-I-Am's problem with the Green Eggs and Ham guy. He just didn't like him. Or put another way, there was no H2H connection!

Even in the first sales book that had an impact on me, *How to Win Friends and Influence People*, nowhere in the book does Dale Carnegie claim that you need to have a relationship with somebody.[18] He talked about the likeability factor. If you are going to persuade prospects that you are interesting enough to win time on

---

17   McCormack, Mark H., Ari Emanuel, and Patrick Whitesell. "What They Still Don't Teach You at Harvard Business School." Amazon. 2015. Accessed October 02, 2021. https://www.amazon.com/What-Teach-Harvard-Business-School/dp/0553345834.

18   Carnegie, Dale. *How to Win Friends Influence People*. Kingswood: Worlds Work, 1913.

their calendar, you need to be likeable. And how does likeability manifest? See Rule #1: Always Maintain Good Balance.

Everyone can drive to a Starbucks window and build rapport with the barista in a matter of forty-five seconds. That's not a relationship. Relationship is an outcome. But there's another factor. What does your approach look like? You may be so worried about building a relationship that you don't do the little things that build rapport, like remember a person's name, or mirror and match how they speak. Or maybe you are disrespectful with their time and tell them you only need a minute...but end up taking five. These are all things that destroy rapport.

The former chairman of a very well-known employee-benefit and insurance agency would specifically ask the front desk person how the visiting salesperson treated her. He knew who he was dealing with when they came in the door based on how that salesperson treated *everyone* in the office, not just him (the decision-maker).

Likeability is a complex factor. If you're going to pull it off sincerely, you need to flex your EQ.

Rule #3: Always have a Winning Attitude

As established earlier in the book, understanding the mindset of the person you want to persuade is the first consideration. When you call a business, an angel investor, a potential donor, or a restaurant manager on a busy Saturday night, you have to expect that they are preoccupied with a million other things. Your job is to break through that veil of distraction. There's a lot more on overcoming prospect preoccupation later in the book. For now, let's focus on the attitude of someone even more important than the buyer...*you*. After all, winning or losing the Super Bowl all begins within the six inches between your own ears.

A winning attitude for selling H2H can be summed up in the following poem:

The Little Black Hen[19]

Said a little red rooster, "Gosh, all hemlock things are tough. Seems the worms are getting scarcer; I cannot find enough. What's become of all the fat ones is a mystery to me. There were thousands throughout the rainy spell. Now, where can they be?"

The old hen heard him; didn't grumble, didn't complain. She'd gone through lots of dry spells. She'd lived through flood and rain. She flew up on a grindstone and gave her claws a whet. And she said, "I've never seen a time when there weren't worms to get."

She picked a new undug spot. The earth was hard and firm. The little rooster jeered, "New ground. That's no place to worm." The old hen just spread her feet. She dug both fast and free. "I must go to the worms," she said, "the worms won't come to me."

The rooster wanly spent his day, through habit, by the ways where the fat worms had passed in squads, back in the rainy days. Nightfall found him supperless, he growled in accents rough, "I'm as hungry as fowl can be, conditions sure are tough." He turned then to the old hen and said, "It's worse for you, for you're not only hungry, but you must be tired too. I rested while I watched for worms so I feel fairly perk, but how are you without worms, too? And after all that work."

The old hen hopped on to her perch and dropped her eyes to sleep and murmured in a drowsy tone, "Young man, hear me and weep. I'm full of worms and I'm happy, I've dined both long and well. The worms were there as always, but I had to dig like hell."

---

19   "The Little Black Hen." Scrapbook.com. Accessed October 02, 2021. https://www.scrapbook.com/poems/doc/6064.html.

Good business leaders, salespeople, and entrepreneurs create an opportunity where one doesn't exist. *This* is why we do what we do. To create something out of nothing, we need to adopt the attitude of the hen. Successful H2H selling means reinforcing an attitude of digging like hell for worms—for opportunities to persuade and influence—because they sure aren't coming to you.

> **Successful H2H selling means reinforcing an attitude of digging like hell for worms—for opportunities to persuade and influence—because they sure aren't coming to you.**

But as important as the previous three rules are, the final rule is the most critical if you want to win the persuasion and influence game.

Rule #4: Know Your Buyer

As the markets shift and your approach to selling H2H changes, you need to understand that the tectonic plates are shifting for the buyer—the person or people you want to persuade—as well. Because of the merging and purging going on in organizations, they are operating much, much leaner. A typical firm with 100 to 500 employees has anywhere from three to five people involved in most buying decisions. That's added to the complexity of the decision-making process. It's made sales much more high stakes and has required salespeople to connect with all sorts of buyer profiles: the technical buyer, the executive buyer, and sometimes the financial buyer.

Now the question has become: Do people want to be sold or do they want to buy? According to CSO Insights, many buyers now want to define their needs on their own before they engage with the sales rep. In fact, 44 percent want to identify a specific solution before even reaching out to a seller.[20] Many of these decisions are being defined internally, which is forcing the salesperson to meet the buyer where they are. Not to mention buyers are facing increasing internal pressure to protect the budget at all costs.

Unfortunately, the fear of loss and failure is driving many buying decisions. My company was working with one of our clients, Fenway Sports Management: Boston Red Sox and Liverpool F.C., during the height of the pandemic regarding a pitch to a consumer product brand. The buyer stated that they did have the budget left to make a deal, but they were still going to wait and see if things changed as it got closer to the end of the year. In a normal market, buyers like that would have been more than willing to spend the money already earmarked in their budget. The philosophy used to be use it or lose it. This new market, however, is unprecedented. It has made your potential buyer much more like the weather in the Midwest—unpredictable. Your goal, rounding out the rules of persuasion and influence, is to convince them that you are someone worth listening to.

These four rules prepare you long before you reach out to a buyer. You need to recognize the heavy lift needed to win time and increase awareness. In a virtual environment, this is even more important because the physical presence is missing. The buyer might not know who you represent, what you have to offer, or what value you bring. Increasing that awareness is more crucial than it was in the past.

---

20   Gerencer, Tom. "200 Sales Statistics [Cold Calling, Follow-up, Closing Rates]." Zety. May 28, 2021.

Insidesales.com says you need a combination of six to eight touches just to get an actual decision-maker on the phone.[21] That doesn't ensure they'll agree to meet with you. Because of the new business reality of today, it's been forecasted that winning time on people's calendars or getting them to pick up the phone isn't getting any easier. Those numbers likely have increased since the pandemic.

Businesspeople and entrepreneurs often say, "I'd do really good if you just put me in front of the right people." What most don't understand is that about 20 to 30 percent of their efforts need to go into creating that opportunity.[22] Successfully playing the persuasion and influence game means following the rules, having the right attitude, and *always* working to be in front of the right people.

That about covers the mirror side of the H2H equation. Now, let's peer through the window and into the tactics needed to reach the opportunities beyond.

. . . .

H2H Reflections

- When it comes to selling H2H, your job exists for one of two reasons:
  - To persuade or influence in the moment
  - To begin the process that will set up a future change in thought or behavior
- Understand the rules of the persuasion and influence game:

---

21   Gerencer, Tom. "200 Sales Statistics [Cold Calling, Follow-up, Closing Rates]." Zety. May 28, 2021.
22   Gerencer, Tom. "200 Sales Statistics [Cold Calling, Follow-up, Closing Rates]." Zety. May 28, 2021.

- o Always maintain a good balance of understanding, credibility, and rapport
- o Relationships are an outcome of H2H connections
- o If you want worms (opportunities), dig like hell
- o Know your potential buyers' mindset and convince them you are someone worth listening to
- How do you rank in your understanding of the rules of persuasion and influence? Have you exercised any or all of them in the past without realizing it? Which one(s)?

CHAPTER SIX:

The Window: The Power of Opinions

• • •

"Nothing draws a crowd quite like a crowd."
—P. T. Barnum

Most people know that P.T. Barnum was considered the greatest showman on earth. What most people don't realize, however, is that he was one of the greatest salesmen on earth as well. He understood the underpinnings of persuasion better than anyone of his time. We're talking about a guy who had an *elephant* plow the front yard of his house in Connecticut right next to the railroad tracks where hundreds of people would pass by daily.[23]

There are several ways to look at someone like P.T. Barnum. His life was painted with charitable deeds as well as controversy.

---

23 "Timeless Sales Tips From P.T. Barnum." Entrepreneur. February 28, 2012. Accessed October 02, 2021. https://www.entrepreneur.com/article/29602.

But in looking at the net effect of his influence over the totality of his life, one thing is for certain: he was a master of persuasion. And for the record, there is no definitive proof that he ever said, "There's a sucker born every minute." To the contrary, he cared deeply about product value and customer satisfaction. He was all for cross-promoting with other businesses that complemented his products. And he never simply pitched his products and just expected the crowds to enjoy them. He *listened* to his customers. He tried to understand their needs. Then he would dial in his offering to fulfill those needs.

> **Social proof is one of the cornerstones of influence and persuasion.**

Barnum knew how to motivate the masses. He understood how to reach the people on the other side of the metaphoric window through the power of other peoples' opinions—a concept of *social proof*—long before Robert Cialdini wrote about it in his 1984 bestseller *Influence: The Psychology of Persuasion*.[24] Social proof has become an area of study that sociologists and psychologists can't get enough of, and it is one of the cornerstones of influence and persuasion. Whether you know it or not, social proof is all around you. Think about this.... have you ever decided to go out to breakfast while on vacation or while you're in any new town? How do you pick a restaurant? Like many, you probably look at how many cars are in the parking lot. Maybe one restaurant only has a car or two, while the other restaurant is packed. Which one do you gravitate towards? Probably the one with all the people.

---

24   Cialdini, R. B. (2007). *Influence: The psychology of persuasion*. New York, NY: Collins.

In fact, social proof is so powerful that you will likely deny logic to be part of the crowd. One fascinating example is the Solomon Asch conformity experiment from 1951.[25] Asch was a respected psychologist that wanted to test the limits of social proof—to show that people are willing to reject their own perception to fit in.

Asch recruited a bunch of male college students to participate in the experiment—what he called a *line judgment task*. Each group was shown images like the ones below:

The participants had to identify which line (A, B, or C) matched the target line on the left. Asch performed the experiment by dividing the participants into groups of eight and had all eight answer the questions with the others in the room. The catch was, only one of the people in each group was actually being tested. The other seven were planted and agreed beforehand as to what their answers would be.

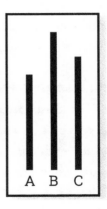

Each plant had to reveal which line was most like the target line, with the real participant going last every time. The correct answer was obvious, just like in the picture. Out of a total of eighteen trials, the plants were told to give wrong answers in twelve of them. During those twelve tests, 75 percent of the real partic-

25   Mcleod, S. (n.d.). Solomon Asch - Conformity Experiment. Retrieved from
      https://www.simplypsychology.org/asch-conformity.html

ipants went with the masses and gave the wrong answer—even though they could clearly see the correct answer!

When Asch asked the real participants why they went with the group, those individuals gave two main reasons:

1. They believed the group was better informed than themselves.
2. They wanted to fit in with the group.

This first reason is extremely important in understanding the bedrock of the Human Sales Factor. Information, or lack thereof, influences our behaviors and decisions. Which means the power of "expert" opinions can drastically influence decision making.

Knowledge is Power

The dissonance in knowledge for the buyer and the seller has played a crucial role in sales for decades—*asymmetric information*—which was briefly mentioned in the Introduction. This occurs when there is an information imbalance, typically in the seller's favor. Whether you are selling a house, a car, a lawnmower, or yourself, you have a distinct advantage. You likely know more about the house than your prospective buyer. You know all the attractive features, but you also know about all the flaws. You know that the neighbors are noisy on the weekends. You know how cold the upstairs gets in the winter. You know that the basement floods with two inches of water after a hard rain.

To combat asymmetric information, many industries require legal disclosures by the seller. This way, the buyer can truly make an informed decision while assessing the actual value of a purchase. But this concept isn't limited to the buying and selling of goods. Doctors, for instance, know more about health and medicine than their patients. The same can be said for lawyers, police officers, personal trainers, home builders—you name the field, and it's likely that asymmetric information exists. But it's not always a bad thing. How would you like to have to go to medical school, law school, dental school, and various trade schools for plumbing, roofing, and electrical, just to live in society?

Becoming an expert in every field imaginable isn't practical or economical, so society has created a process of checks and balances so people can specialize in certain industries, serve others, and make a living. But there is something that has really leveled the playing field in the past couple of decades: *technology*. Today, buyers have instant access to as much information about a particular product, service, or person as they can possibly consume. The problem is, while knowledge is power, too much knowledge can be dangerously overwhelming.

That's why the Human Sales Factor requires trust, rapport, and credibility, not just knowledge. And that's why the subjects of the Asch experiment listed *two* main reasons for selecting the line that they could clearly see was incorrect. Now let's unpack the second reason: They wanted to fit in with the group. This reason makes a powerful statement in terms of buying and selling—humans are hardwired to follow.

Following the Herd

Let's bounce back to our restaurant example for a second. The reason you're likely to head for the one with all the cars in the parking lot is the information you're receiving. Humans are social creatures, hardwired to look to one another for evidence that something might be better, nicer, cleaner, safer.

This pertains to survival instincts. You see an empty parking lot at a restaurant and automatically think, "Maybe the food will make me sick." Who wants to be the lone gazelle at a watering hole? Nobody. Maybe that restaurant with two cars in the lot just opened. Maybe they have better food at better prices, but poor marketing. "Doesn't matter," says your survival instinct. You want to be with the masses. The group must know better than you.

Think about when you go shopping. When you're in a shoe store for example, you have the ability to directly compare one shoe to another and determine which is better. There's not a whole lot of outside influence on which shoes you buy. Or, if you're at the mall doing a little clothes shopping, you can try on a shirt, feel the fabric, the quality, the fit. However, when you're shopping online, deciding which shoe or shirt is best is a lot more difficult. So, what do you do? Read the reviews. When it comes to buying something online, we *feel compelled* to rely on outside opinions to make a final decision since we don't have the product in hand to examine it ourselves.

Before you buy those shoes online, you look at reviews to see what other people think of the fit and quality. Even if you personally like the style, what others say can ultimately sway your opinion. Why? Because we assume they have more information about the product than we do. After all, they've taken the plunge to buy it and experience it.

What do you think would happen if a hybrid version of this social proof influence popped up? What if brick-and-mortar businesses displayed the reviews of all the products they sold? It would change the way we shop forever. The thing is, this is already happening. Have you ever whipped out your phone at Best Buy to make sure the new gadget you're buying has great reviews? You are not alone. One study found that 50 percent of shoppers use their smartphones while shopping in stores to research products before buying them.[26]

As you can imagine, when used correctly, social proof can be a very powerful tool for influencing someone to buy whatever it is you are selling. Highlighting the popularity of products or service can drive a buyer's confidence that what you have is what they need. Social proof works the other way around,

Negative reviews can stop an average of 40 percent of buyers from wanting to do business with the offending company.

too. It's a very powerful tool to influence someone to give *you* something you want or need.

Let's say you're at the airport and the flight isn't full. You want an upgrade to first class. Do you have any bargaining power? Actually, you do. In today's business world, customer satisfaction is king. Most businesses realize that an unhappy customer will eventually lead to an unhappy review—which is read by everyone in the universe. Current research says that negative reviews can stop an average of 40 percent of buyers from wanting to do business with the offending company.[27]

So, in a sense, when you try to get that upgrade to first class, you're technically selling. "This is my favorite airline. Because the flight isn't quite full this time, would I be able to get bumped up to first class? I'd be happy to leave a really positive review or take a survey." Boom! How many gate agents are going to turn that

---

26 Big Commerce. *What Influences a Purchase Decision*. 2020. https://www.bigcommerce.com/what-influences-a-purchase-decision-infographic/

27 Murphy, Rosie. "Local Consumer Review Survey: How Customer Reviews Affect Behavior." BrightLocal. August 31, 2021. Accessed October 02, 2021. https://www.brightlocal.com/research/local-consumer-review-survey/.

down? If it's not a fully booked flight, not many. Plus, you are appealing to that other social condition we're all subject to—helping one another. You get your upgrade while the gate agent gets their review and feels good about themselves.

Remember, selling H2H isn't about moving a product or service, it's about moving *people*. That means *you* have the power to influence others through the rapport you build, which ultimately drives a change in behavior. Credibility yields trust, which ultimately puts you on the path to persuasion. And that's why your personal brand is more important to leverage than ever.

The Power of the Personal Brand

Believe it or not, branding is not simply for companies, celebrities, and social media influencers. Think of your personal brand as your public identity. Your brand is your resume, how you write an email, your social media profile. It's a way to convey who you are, your trustworthiness, and your credibility to people who don't know you well in a short amount of time. And because we are all salespeople, your ability to persuade relies on your reputation.

> You can't just turn on the charm when you want something from someone. H2H selling requires that you are always authentic in your connection with others.

Would you say you are generally known as an optimist? Do you keep your promises? Are you typically on time and dependable? Are you friendly? Easygoing? Does your LinkedIn picture look professional? Do you even have a picture up on LinkedIn? All these attributes come together to define your brand—either by design or default. You can't just turn on the charm when you want something from someone. H2H selling requires that you are always authentic in your connection with others. Your repetition is your reputation.

Brand Builders Group founder and CEO, Rory Vaden, commissioned an independent research firm to conduct a study on personal branding.[28] The data showed three main things:

1. Personal branding is the future.
2. Personal branding is highly profitable.
3. Personal branding is a trust accelerator.

As Rory says, "Personal branding is simply the digitization of reputation." With a personal brand, comes the power to influence and persuade exponentially. We trust personal brands every day. That's why endorsement deals with athletes are worth hundreds of millions of dollars. Because people trust people they see all the time, and who others know and love.

Remember, no matter how awesome your product or service might be, it's still critical to make the H2H connection. That's why when you ask yourself whether it's more important that the brand you represent has rapport and credibility or that you have rapport and credibility, the answer is always *you*. Your personal brand matters first and foremost. People buy from people first. How do you get instant credibility and rapport so people are willing to stop whatever it is they are doing and listen to what you have to say? A little tactic called Shock and Awe Persuasion.

---

28 Vaden, Rory. "Influential Leader Blog." Rory Vaden Official Site. Accessed October 02, 2021. http://www.roryvaden.com/blog.

Shock and Awe Persuasion

You might recall the popularity of the term Shock and Awe during the Iraq War, when allied forces overwhelmed Bagdad and neighboring cities with incredible volleys of missiles and bombs during the initial invasion. Historically speaking, this concept has been around for about, oh, *four thousand years*. It's based on the military tactic of coming in with so much force and firepower that you overwhelm your opponent to the point they just sit down and give up. Genghis Khan used it. The ancient Romans used it. In fact, Alexander the Great used it all the time. Whenever he went into a new territory he wanted to conquer, he would deploy massive amounts of troops and overrun the local population, killing hundreds—if not thousands—and burning everything to the ground. Needless to say, all the surrounding towns would give up without a fight. Every time. Why? Because of Alexander the Great's ruthless reputation—his personal brand.

88 percent of consumers trust online reviews as much as personal recommendations.

This is not to suggest that you destroy those you hope to persuade or influence. Instead, Shock and Awe Persuasion is designed to blow minds. Some of the ways that marketing and sales companies try to move the masses with Shock and Awe Persuasion include:

1. Lots of Positive Reviews

Are you among the 70 percent of Americans who seek out opinions and review sites before making purchases?[29] Do you

---

29   "70% of Americans Seek out Opinions before Purchasing." Mintel. June 03, 2015. Accessed October 02, 2021. https://www.mintel.com/press-centre/social-and-lifestyle/seven-in-10-americans-seek-out-opinions-before-making-purchases.

ignore the one-, two-, and three-star reviews on Yelp, and instead only go for the restaurants with four- or five-stars?

A company called BrightLocal says that 88 percent of consumers trust online reviews as much as personal recommendations.[30] On average, consumers don't just trust the first reviews they see. They hit up two to three different review sites before deciding.

. . . .

Interesting Stats on the Power of Reviews[31]

- 93 percent of consumers used the Internet to find a local business in the last year.

- 87 percent of consumers read online reviews for local businesses in 2020–up from 81 percent in 2019.

- 31 percent of consumers say they read more reviews in 2020 because of COVID-19, while 34 percent read fewer.

- The industries in which consumers are most likely to read reviews include 1) restaurants, 2) hotels, 3) medical, 4) automotive, and 5) clothing stores.

- The most important review factors include 1) star rating, 2) legitimacy, 3) recency, 4) sentiment, and 5) quantity.

- Only 48 percent of consumers would consider using a business with a rating of fewer than four stars.

- 73 percent of consumers only pay attention to reviews written in the last month.

- 72 percent of U.S. consumers have written a review for a local business—a big jump from 66 percent in 2019.

---

30 Murphy, Rosie. "Local Consumer Review Survey: How Customer Reviews Affect Behavior." BrightLocal. August 31, 2021.

31 Gerencer, Tom. "200 Sales Statistics [Cold Calling, Follow-up, Closing Rates]." Zety. May 28, 2021.

- When writing a review, 20 percent of consumers expect to receive a response within one day.
- Consumers are most likely to look at Google My Business for local business reviews, but trust the Better Business Bureau the most.

. . . .

What do all these stats mean? They mean that tons of reviews provide a very effective form of persuasion. Shock and Awe people with your positive reviews. They are looking!

2. Lots of Customer Testimonials

Just saying you have an awesome product or service isn't the most effective strategy to persuade people to buy what you're selling. On the other hand, lots of testimonials from happy customers…that's Shock and Awe Persuasion in action.

If you had to name one industry that does this better than almost any other, what would it be? If you said weight-loss, you are correct. Think of all the before-and-after testimonials of people who lost weight, gained muscle, improved their relationships, and increased their self-esteem just by counting calories. Or taking two scientifically designed pills before every meal. Or eating a specialized protein bar. Or subscribing to a particular weight-loss app.

Those ads are damn convincing, aren't they? Admit it, you've bought at least one weight loss product at some point in your life. It's not a multibillion-dollar industry for nothing. It just goes to show that evidence displayed through customer testimonials is an extremely powerful form of persuasion.

3. Name Dropping

We've already established that most people rely on the masses to make decisions about what to purchase. Testimonials provide compelling evidence of the positive results just waiting for you if you buy the product or service being advertised. And what happens when an influencer—a singer, Hollywood star, pro-athlete—adds their two-cents?

> **Content from influencers earns more than 8 times the engagement rate of content shared directly from brands.**

Well, according to an influencer marketing study, a lot. Businesses are averaging $6.50 for every $1 spent on influencer marketing, with the top 13 percent earning $20 or more.[32] Influencer marketing is particularly effective on social media. Check out the following stats:[33]

- Twitter users have an increase of 5.2 times the purchase intent after seeing promotional content from influencers.
- 49 percent of users rely on recommendations from influencers on Twitter.
- 40 percent of people say they've purchased a product online after seeing it used by an influencer on social media.
- Content from influencers earns more than 8 times the engagement rate of content shared directly from brands.

---

32 Murphy, Rosie. "Local Consumer Review Survey: How Customer Reviews Affect Behavior." BrightLocal. August 31, 2021.

33 Swant, Marty. "Twitter Says Users Now Trust Influencers Nearly as Much as Their Friends." Adweek. May 10, 2016. Accessed October 02, 2021. https://www.adweek.com/performance-marketing/twitter-says-users-now-trust-influencers-nearly-much-their-friends-171367/.

Now this doesn't mean you need to name drop JLo or Elton John to persuade someone to buy what you are selling. An influencer could also be someone with an active social media following or an industry expert—just about anyone who has built-in credibility and influence over the person or people you're trying to reach.

To show the power of influencers, check this out: Facebook founder, Mark Zuckerberg, was out grilling steaks one day and posted about how thrilled he was with a grilling thermometer called iGrill. The result? The iGrill website crashed with 1000 visitors per minute, and their brand awareness skyrocketed a million-fold.

> **Adding recognizable logos from customers for social proof can increase your conversion rate by 400 percent!**

To be sure, influencers don't just have to be people; influencers can be popular brands with affiliation to your brand. In fact, adding recognizable logos from customers for social proof can increase your conversion rate by 400 percent![34]

4. Show Off to Shine

One of the surest ways to use Shock and Awe Persuasion is to tout any awards or recognition you received relating to your product or service. This third-party validation holds tremendous value to persuade and influence. In fact, a former ecommerce company called Bag Servant once did a study to see if adding one of their awards to the top of their website pages would result in better

---

34 "How We Increased the Conversion Rate of Voices.com by over 400%: Conversion Rate Experts." January 21, 2010. Accessed October 02, 2021. https://conversion-rate-experts.com/voices-case-study/.

conversions.[35] They created two sites: a control site and a new site. The control site had a button to follow them on Twitter, along with their follower count. The new site replaced the Twitter info with a WOW badge—an award given annually from a well-known businesswoman.

The website with the award at the top crushed the control version with an increased conversion rate of 90 percent!

And don't forget about good old-fashioned media. Showcasing any positive media attention from notable outlets is another form of recognition that is sure to resonate with those you are trying to reach. After all, if it's in the news, it must be true!

The point of Shock and Awe Persuasion is to wow people into wanting to connect with you. When you rely on the science of persuasion, there is a high likelihood that a person will at least grant you a few minutes to talk to them. Alexander the Great relied on Shock and Awe and social proof to conquer most of the known world. Just think what would have happened if he hadn't.

He may have gone down in history as Alexander the Status Quo.

• •

H2H Reflections

- Social proof is scientifically proven and hardwired into our brains. Use it!
- Personal branding is fundamental in creating a major impact in a short amount of time.

---

35 "Bag Servant Increased Conversions By 72%: VWO Success Stories." Website. May 04, 2021. Accessed October 02, 2021. https://vwo.com/success-stories/bag-servant/.

- Leverage the power of Shock and Awe Persuasion by utilizing the following:
  - o   Positive reviews
  - o   Customer testimonials
  - o   Influencer name dropping
  - o   Showing off your awards and recognition
- Have you ever leveraged Shock and Awe Persuasion without realizing it? Which influencers could you lean on for support in your world?

• •

CHAPTER SEVEN:
Presence and Presentation

• • •

*"The single biggest problem in communication
is the illusion it has taken place."*
-George Bernard Shaw

If you've ever watched the show, *Shark Tank*, you know that the panel can be ruthless when evaluating a start-up's potential. However, as I mentioned earlier in the book, the Sharks don't always buy into the most viable product or service—they buy into the *human* making the pitch.

Case in point: In Season 3, Episode 9, of this popular ABC program, Tower Paddle Board founder, Stephan Aarstol, appeared on the show to garner a $150,000 investment in exchange for 10 percent equity. Paddle boarding is a popular pastime for many, and Aarstol's boards retail at about half the price of competitor products. Sounds like a decent investment opportunity, right? The only problem was that Aarstol was so nervous he started babbling and bungling his way through the opening of his pitch.

The Sharks looked confused. More than that, they looked unimpressed. But there was something about Aarstol—a likeability factor—that kept the Sharks intrigued. Daymond started asking questions that ultimately revealed Aarstol's expertise in paddle boards. Before long, Aarstol was in a groove, and the Sharks were throwing him offers. Eventually, Mark Cuban sealed the deal with a $150,000 investment and 30 percent equity stake. And as of 2018, Tower Paddle Boards cleared over $30 million in sales.[36]

> **Likeability is a tremendous indicator when communicating H2H.**

Stephen Aarstol may not have been the most polished speaker, but he had the likeability factor. As it turns out, likeability is a tremendous indicator when communicating H2H.

Stage Presence Is Everything

An associate professor at UCL School of Management, Chia-Jung Tsay, conducted a study where she asked 1,855 participants to predict the winners of various venture capital pitch competitions.[37] These participants ranged from angel investors and experienced entrepreneurs to start-up founders with little to no business experience. They reviewed contestant presentations in a variety of manners, including silent videos, transcripts, audio recordings only, and video and audio recordings combined.

36   Basnett, Neetesh. "Tower Paddle Boards Surfs to $30 million in Sales After 'Shark Tank'". Dallas Business Journal. Aug 15, 2018. Accessed October 02, 2021. https://www.bizjournals.com/dallas/news/2018/08/15/tower-paddle-boards-surfs-to-30m-in-sales-after.html.

37   Martinez, Juan. "In Entrepreneurial Pitches, Stage Presence Is Everything." Harvard Business Review. September 17, 2021. Accessed October 02, 2021. https://hbr.org/2021/09/in-entrepreneurial-pitches-stage-presence-is-everything.

The results were mind-boggling. Professor Tsay found that the participants could most accurately predict which people were awarded the funding from the VCs when they watched the silent videos of the pitch. Even if the content of the pitch was genius, enthusiasm won the day. And it only took participants a few seconds to guess which person pitching was going to win the funding from the VCs.

As Professor Tsay recounted:

"Most investors would say that when they're deciding which start-ups to back, they focus on interesting ideas, talented founders, and substantive business plans. But across 12 studies I found that people could predict VC funding decisions based not on the actual content of entrepreneurs' pitches but on how they were presented, especially body language and facial expressions. Often people watching the silent videos took only a few seconds to correctly identify which pitches had been favored by the investors. In my studies the visuals influenced judgment more than words or other information did."[38]

There's an old adage known by trial attorneys about how to win a case every time. If you have data, pound on the data. If you have evidence, pound on the evidence. And if you don't have either, pound on the desk.

Clearly enthusiasm goes a long way in communicating H2H. Those pitching and winning over the VCs proved this. Like Stephen Aarstol, they had their soft skills down. As mentioned earlier, these are no longer a luxury but a necessity in our H2H interactions. Mastering them is critical if you ever hope to persuade someone to think or behave differently.

---

38   Martinez, Juan. "In Entrepreneurial Pitches, Stage Presence Is Everything." Harvard Business Review. September 17, 2021.

So, what are these soft skills anyway, and how do they work?

The Science of "Soft Skills"

At the end of the day, what are known as "soft skills" are driven by EQ. The higher the EQ, the more polished the soft skills are likely to be. These are the tools used to wield the power of persuasion and interact effectively with others. Research has even found that those who have strong soft skills make an average of $29,000 more per year![39]

Soft skills can be sorted into three distinct groups. The first is personal effectiveness—how you come across to others. Are you confident and able to convey your thoughts clearly? Do you make a good first impression? The next group is your ability to interact with others. Are you perceptive? Are you empathetic? Can you read the room and adjust accordingly? And the last group is the ability to inspire people. Are you a connector? A leader? Can you de-escalate toxic situations?

Here are some of the more well-known soft skills:

- Master communicator
- Great conversationalist
- High likability
- Highly motivated
- Active listener
- Approachable
- Knowledgeable
- Open-minded

---

39 "10 Essential People Skills You Need to Succeed." Science of People. June 22, 2020. Accessed October 02, 2021. https://www.scienceofpeople.com/people-skills/.

- Dependable
- Adaptable
- Good sense of humor

Knowing the soft skills needed to persuade and influence is just the first step. Adopting and refining these skills in your own personality is critical. But to do so, you first need to understand how the human brain processes H2H communication. Between 80 and 90 percent of the information that our brain processes is visual.40 Not only

We are hardwired to consume visual information.

that, but two-thirds of the brain's electrical activity is dedicated to vision. That means we are hardwired to consume visual information. This goes a long way in explaining Professor Tsay's results.

Using a visual can enhance your presentation if it is done correctly. But don't use a visual for the pure sake of using a visual. Today, technology is a major part of our world, and we often incorporate technology into our presentations. Be cognizant of the fact that technology-based visuals can make a concept harder to understand. If you incorporate a visual—any visual—make sure it adds to the presentation and helps clarify your message.

Another factor in how our brain processes H2H communication is our inherent love of storytelling. According to *The Scientific American*, our brains process personal stories differently than when receiving other forms of oral information.[41] The same can be

---

40 Udomon, Iboro, Xiong, Chuyee, et al. Visual, Audio, and Kinesthetic Effects on Memory Retention and Recall [Web log post]. 2013. Retrieved from http://jass. neuro.wisc.edu/2013/01/Group%203.Udomon.Final%20Submission.pdf

41 Hsu, Jeremy. "The Secrets of Storytelling: Why We Love a Good Yarn." Scientific American. Accessed October 02, 2021. https://www.scientificamerican.com/ article/the-secrets-of-storytelling/.

said for how our brain processes two-way conversations. There is

How you want to be sold is how you need to sell.

a phenomenon known as neural coupling where your brain activity begins to mirror the other person during a conversation.[42]

Always remember, how you want to be sold is how you need to sell. Learn to see the world through your prospective buyer's eyes. That's the only way to make a lasting impression.

But before making a lasting impression, you need to make the first one...

The All-Important First Impression

Every time you meet someone, you make a good impression or a bad one. Period. And a bad impression is a lot harder to undo than you think. An article published in *Perspectives on Psychological Science* detailed an experiment where participants were told about a company that was in the process of hiring a new CEO.[43] The participants learned that one of the candidates requested an expensive marble table as a perk for the job. Guess what happened? The participants found this request so appalling that they "reported a preference for paying an additional $1 million in salary to a different job candidate just to avoid hiring a candidate whose salary request included a $40,000 marble table."

---

42 Stephens, Greg J., Silbert, Lauren J., and Hasson, Uri. "Speaker–Listener Neural Coupling Underlies Successful Communication." PDF file. April 30, 2010. *https://pnas.org/content/107/32/14425.full.pdf*

43 Uhlmann, E. L., Pizarro, D. A., & Diermeier, D. (2015). A person-centered approach to moral judgment. *Perspectives on Psychological Science, 10*(1), 72-81. doi: 10.1177/1745691614556679

Not only are bad first impressions long-lasting, but they are also unequivocally more difficult to forgive. In another study, five randomized experiments revealed that humans hold onto a poor judgement of someone after observing a social or moral faux pas much longer than a good impression.[44] The researchers found that it takes many redemptive impressions to erase one bad impression, while only one bad impression to tarnish a good impression.

Developing an impression—especially a good first impression—gives the message momentum and credibility. We need that momentum to persuade and influence more effectively. And creating a positive impression is done within the opening of your message. It should be strong and build trust with the receiver of your message.

> **Developing an impression—especially a good first impression—gives the message momentum and credibility.**

But remember, making the right impression doesn't just correspond to the first impression. Throughout an entire interaction with those you hope to connect with and persuade, make sure to reflect the right image, *always*. Think about that word for a moment: *in all ways*. This gives credibility. As people get to know you, they go through various stages to create impressions of you.

44　Klein, N., & O'Brien, E. (2016). The Tipping Point of Moral Change: When Do Good and Bad Acts Make Good and Bad Actors?. *Social Cognition, 34*(2), 149. doi: 10.1521/soco.2016.34.2.149

CONTROL YOUR IMPRESSION

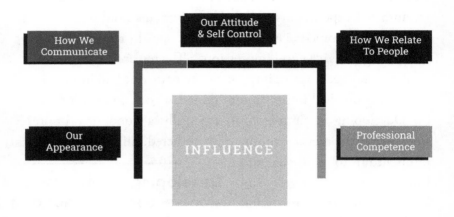

Let's take a look at the various stages of the impression we make:

Your Appearance

Do you look like you are serious and nicely groomed, or do you look like a beach bum with a margarita in your hand and a cigarette dangling out of your mouth?

How You Communicate

Just because you are pitching to your brother on an idea doesn't mean you don't have to be clear, concise, and professional.

Your Attitude & Self Control

Show that you have a positive attitude and you're excited about what you do. But make sure to exhibit self-control. See the chapter on EQ.

How You Relate to People

Try to understand who your buyer is and try to relate to them based on their interests. Find common ground.

Professional Competence

Make sure you know what you're talking about and show it. Making a good impression is important in ensuring credibility, but credibility goes beyond that first impression and leads to the *lasting impression.*

Relevance

If the person you are trying to persuade or influence feels that the information is not relevant or doesn't get to the point fast enough, they will stop listening.

Here are the Lucky 13—the tactics needed to supercharge the delivery of any message:

1. Use the buyer's name.
2. Play yourself down, not up!
3. Say "we" - not "you".
4. Don't talk with a reproachful voice.
5. Talk in terms of the listeners' interests.
6. Have a good time delivering the message.
7. Don't apologize.
8. Appeal to the nobler emotions of the listener.
9. If hoping to pitch something significant, unless absolutely necessary, don't write out the pitch. Instead, make brief notes of the interesting things to mention.
10. Never memorize a pitch word-for-word. All it takes is forgetting one sentence and everything can fly off the rails.
11. Know far more about the subject than you can use.

12. Don't imitate others. Be yourself!
13. Look in the mirror—even though you are not purposely scowling, you may have a default look that is not as approachable as your smiling face.

Your ability to connect and persuade—making that reach through the window—starts with your presence. Next up: your messaging.

• •

H2H Reflections

- Enthusiasm and likeability are critical in communicating H2H.
- Soft skills are driven by EQ. The higher the EQ, the more polished the soft skills are likely to be.
- Soft skills can be sorted into three distinct groups: personal effectiveness, your ability to interact with others, and your ability to inspire people.
- Bad first impressions are long-lasting, but they are also more difficult to forgive. Don't make them!
- Control your first impression by:
  - Polishing your appearance (visuals matter!)
  - Being aware of how you communicate
  - Being mindful of your attitude
  - Relating to others
  - Showing you are professionally competent
  - Staying relevant and on topic

• •

CHAPTER EIGHT:

Message and Momentum

• • •

"My life is my message."
- Mahatma Gandhi

It was late in the season when Adam and Ben finally got together to play a round of golf. They had been coworkers for months, but never socialized outside of the job before. Neither are great golfers. Being a bit of a gambler and wanting to keep things interesting, Adam says to Ben just before they tee off, "Hey, let's make a bet on who wins each hole."

Ben shrugs. "Nah, I don't like to gamble."

"Look, it's just for fun," says Adam. "Let's make it just a penny for the first hole and we can go from there."

"One penny?" Ben laughs. "Sure, I think I can afford that."

Ben ends up paring that first hole and becomes a penny richer.

"You want to bet a penny again? Let's double down," says Adam.

"What's another penny to risk?" says Ben, and they play the next hole.

As luck would have it, Ben wins again. Two cents richer. Then Adam suggests they keep going—double or nothing.

"We're only talking pennies anyway," says Adam. "When's the last time you even *saw* a penny. Hole three is worth a measly four cents."

Again Ben wins, and at four cents, he's feeling pretty cocky. "Let's just keep doubling for the rest of the round."

They shake on it. Hole four is worth eight cents, and Adam takes that one. But Ben's not worried because he's planning on taking Adam at hole five. Boom, he wins sixteen cents. Hole six is up next, which Adam wins for thirty-two cents. Ben is pissed, but they're not even at a dollar. Yet.

Hole seven Ben wins sixty-four cents. Hole eight Adam wins $1.28. Hole nine Adam wins again, a whopping $2.56. Not even the cost of a Starbucks latte. But Ben is pretty competitive, so he focuses hard and takes Adam on hole ten. $5.12. Now they are in the betting range of the latte. At hole eleven, Adam crushes Ben for $10.24. *Hell, that's a Starbucks and an Egg McMuffin,* thinks Ben.

But Ben makes an incredible comeback and pars hole twelve to land $20.48. Now things are getting real. Ben pars hole thirteen, too, earning a cool $40.96. Hole fourteen is a par five, and Adam pulls off a birdie for $81.92.

Now Ben is starting to smack-talk because the pressure is on. Adam remains cool, however, and chips one in on hole fifteen, 20 yards out for $163.84. Ben doesn't let that get him, though. He finally birdies on hole sixteen for $327.68.

Two holes left, and both guys are starting to sweat. Ben flubs his drive, which costs him hole seventeen and $655.36. And then there is one hole left, good old number eighteen, a par four. Ben hits a killer drive. But so does Adam. Ben pitches 80 yards to the green…and so does Adam. They both have a ten-footer to sink. Ben gives Adam honors to putt first, and he pulls up short by a foot. Ben, however, drains his ball right in for a final victory and a purse of $1,310.72.

That's the Law of Compounding Interest. Just like the bets on the holes compounded more quickly than expected, the small moves you make when trying to persuade and influence add up. It doesn't seem like a lot is happening at first, but compounding interest one of the most powerful forces because of how quickly the momentum builds.

It takes compounding interest—literally and figuratively—to influence a change in thought or behavior. And the key to building that kind of momentum in persuasion lies within the numbers 7, 21, and 63. In fact, these numbers are vital to the Human Sales Factor. Why, you ask? Keep reading.

Lucky Number 7

Remember, those we hope to persuade and influence will likely see you as an interruption. Their mindset is preoccupied. They'll hear your first few words, listen to your voicemail, or check your email, and in a nano-second think:

- How is this person different?
- Why would I want to talk to this person vs. someone else?
- Is this worth my time?
- Does this conversation have value for me?

Even if you can set yourself apart, are you flexible enough to see the world from their perspective? How well do you understand their role? Are they a key decision-maker or influencer? Can they give you information or a referral?

Why is the number 7 so important to H2H communication? Let's say you want to make an outbound call to connect with someone and set up a meeting. You only have 7 seconds to get favorable attention—and 7 seconds goes a lot quicker than you'd think. By the time you've led with your name, where you are from, and "how are you?", 7 seconds is long gone. In that time, you haven't really created any value or differentiated yourself.

You only have 7 seconds to get favorable attention—and 7 seconds goes a lot quicker than you'd think

If you lead with your own name, you likely haven't caught someone's attention as effectively as you could by catching them off guard. Instead:

- Could you ask a question to verify their name?
- Could you educate them on something that would be important to them?
- Could you use some of the information you have about them to get them to open up?
- Could you appeal to their humanity and ask them for help?

Because they're deciding in a nano-second if you are worth their time, 7 seconds is all you have to get lucky. So why not lead off with the sweetest sound in any language: someone's name. Using someone's name is at the root of connecting with them. They feel known, respected, identified.

If you say, "Hi, this is Corey Smith from down the street. How are you?" you just wasted 7 seconds and ended with a knee-jerk question. Even though your intent is good, you really don't care how they are. So, guess what? You'll get a knee-jerk answer. Every time. You'll get the compulsory, "Fine," because now they've checked out without building any sort of connection.

When communicating H2H, you need to use a compliment or say something interesting. Remember, your buyer is a person, and you get people's attention by talking about things they are interested in. And here's a news flash…they are not interested in you! Otherwise, they would have responded to a previous email or call and said, "Corey, how the hell are you? So glad you called."

Since you probably are not getting those responses, you might have to talk about something that interests them. Like themselves. In fact, you could ask a really cutting-edge question. Remember that a sale is a series of yeses. What do you think your buyer will say if you call them up and ask, "Is this Barbara?"

The sweetest sound in any language: someone's name.

Now imagine that you not only ask that first question and get the rhetorical "yes," but now you ask their last name. "Barbara Johnson?" Boom, another yes. Depending on who you are calling, you might then say, "I understand you're in charge of charitable giving for your company?" Even though it seems redundant and obvious, what do you think they're going to say?

Suddenly, within 7 seconds, you just got three yeses! This may be considered low-hanging fruit, but when you are selling, you need to generate psychological momentum. Getting the prospect to say yes over and over again puts you at a positive advantage and primes them for being agreeable.

For all you readers who are really uncomfortable and thinking, "But I haven't introduced myself yet," please don't confuse being at an in-person event (remember those?) with trying to connect with someone you want to persuade or influence. Here, you just want to get their attention.

21 to 63 Seconds:

If you can sway a person out of preoccupation in those first 7 seconds, you only have the next 21 seconds to generate interest. This is your time to make magic happen. You'll create more interest by focusing on the opportunities, consequences, and outcomes of the product or service because you know that is what is most important—not the product or service itself. Asking a value-based question or making a statement of interest to convince them you are someone worth listening to should be your goal every single time you have the opportunity to connect with anyone!

Let's consider the following example:

When the new version of the iPad Pro was released, I went into the Apple Store to get some information about the new model. The first thing the salesperson asked was, "Did you have an iPad before?"

"Yes," I replied.

The salesperson then asked: "Did you hate the keyboard?"

"Yes."

"Did you hate it because it took like five minutes to get the words up on the screen?"

"Exactly!"

"Did you wish your old iPad worked more like your iPhone?"

"Yes," I said.

The salesperson replied: "The cool thing is, the exact reason why you didn't like your old iPad is the reason why you'll love the new iPad Pro!"

This interaction was all about how the new iPad functions, not about the actual product or me as the buyer. The conversation lasted less than 21 seconds and I walked out with the new iPad Pro.

You need to creatively engage a person in 7 seconds. Then you need to focus on the outcomes that matter most in the next 21 seconds. And if you make it past that hurdle, you may be lucky enough to win just over a minute of their time—even 63 seconds—to get them to acknowledge that you are worth listening to. Those 63 seconds could be the difference in you being a priority amidst all the noise. Because remember, no one is sitting by the phone waiting for your unsolicited call. Sometimes they're not even there for your scheduled phone call. People are busy. They have things that they need to get done, especially if they are in any kind of decision-making capacity. Once you break their preoccupation and get their attention, you have to build their interest. And to keep up the momentum beyond 63 seconds, you can't just keep talking.

> You need to creatively engage a person in 7 seconds. Then you need to focus on the outcomes that matter most in the next 21 seconds.

You also need to *listen*.

The Art of Listening

Have you ever thought about how you listen? This is important in connecting with and persuading others in thought or action. The ability to demonstrate good listening skills allows one to be more influential, whether during a virtual call or a face-to-face meeting. And like delivering the message, there are different levels of listening:

LEVELS OF LISTENING

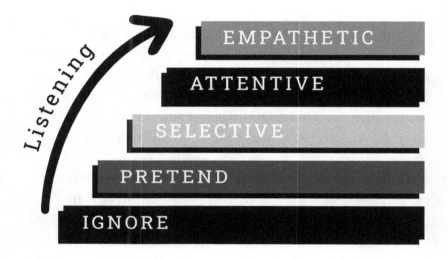

As the diagram shows, listening can range from flat out ignoring the other person to being wholly empathetic. When trying to persuade someone, make sure to constantly check that your listening level is tracking toward the top. This is an awareness that requires practice to be perfect. But the good news is that most people can be aware of their listening level because they know what it's like to be on the receiving end of a sales pitch.

Think about this: have you ever had someone ignore you when you wanted to add a point to what they are saying? Doesn't feel good, does it? Do you pick up when people are pretending to listen to your opinion? How about when they dial in to what you are saying selectively? What about when someone is leaning into what you are saying with authentic empathy?

So now that you know how to listen, let's get back to your messaging. Communicating H2H is not just about the words you say. *How* you say those words is equally important.

Delivery is Everything

When you build up momentum in your messaging, your power of persuasion and influence is unstoppable. But no matter how great the message, if it's not delivered properly, you'll never get the desired results. Business leaders run into this issue all the time. Never thought of a CEO or COO as a salesperson? Well, they are. They need to be able to sell their ideas and visions to their teams constantly. Researchers Tannenbaum and Schmidt created a system to identify the different leadership styles for delivering messages while engaging the power of persuasion.[45]

---

45 "Tannenbaum-Schmidt Leadership Continuum." *Expert Program Management*, 13 Nov. 2018. https://expertprogrammanagement.com/2018/11/tannenbaum-schmidt-leadership-continuum/.

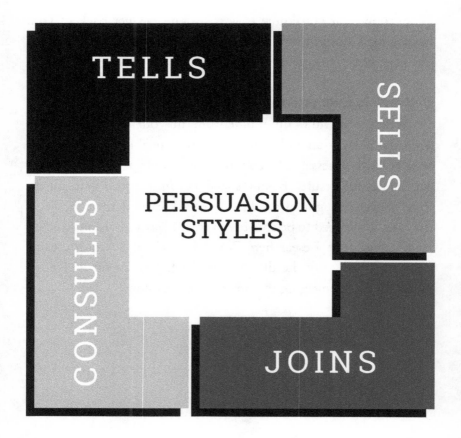

Tells

This leadership style is all about bowling the recipient(s) over with information and forcing them to make a decision. These leaders identify the problem, announce the solution, then expect a decision with no opportunity for participation.

Sells

This leadership style embodies the iconic salesperson in the familiar sense of the word. These leaders identify the problem, submit a decision, but recognize the possibility of resistance.

These leaders are masters at overcoming objections, likely because they've already considered them.

Consults

This style of leadership identifies the problem but does not propose a direct solution without the buy-in from others. They thrive on participation and direct input from others. Then, they tailor their solution.

Joins

Leaders who employ this style identify both the problem and the limits within which a decision can be made. They may recommend bringing in others to support buy-in. They are willing to compromise their ask for the good of the group.

So, which one of these leadership styles reflect how you deliver your message? Whichever one you just said in your mind, you are wrong! To effectively lead others, you need to tailor your message and your leadership style *situationally*. Remember Read-Offense? This is where you apply that strategy—to adapt to the persuasion situation you are faced with.

Back in my door-to-door selling days, I had a presentation memorized by heart for Rainbow® Cleaning System. It went something like this:

"The amazing thing about Rainbow® vacuums is they don't use a traditional filter. With other vacuums, the head sucks up dirt into a bag through a fabric-based micron filter. As you can imagine, over time the dirt ends up clogging the pores—no matter how micro they are—which stresses out the motor and reduces the efficiency of the vacuum. But with Rainbow® vacuum cleaners, their filter is water-based. When the particles of dirt are sucked up, they hit the water and get stuck. Wet dirt is heavy and won't ever get pulled into the bag. Therefore, with a Rainbow® vacuum, you never have to worry about your filter clogging, which wears down your motor and ends in poor performance."

The leadership style you model after is nothing but a filter through which your buyer will hear your message. Selling points can get clogged up quickly if the right filter isn't applied to the right person in the right situation.

Check Your Filter

Think of your filter as your assumptions, your viewpoints, your biases, the context of the situation, your relationship to the person you hope to influence—all the variables that threaten to impact your message.

FILTERS

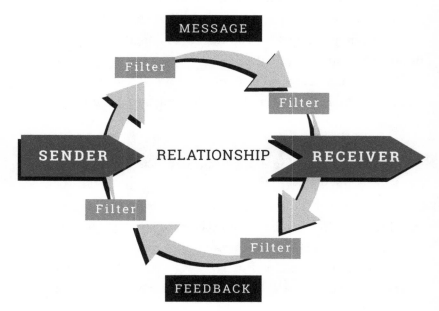

You may have the greatest opportunity in the world for someone, but if you recently learned they lost a loved one to cancer, you may need to apply a different filter to your delivery. You may approach your brother for a donation to your favorite charity differently than your sister. If you just saw the gate agent at the airport deal with a difficult customer, you need to consider their mindset before waltzing in with a request to be bumped up to first class.

On the flip side, you need to understand that the people you are communicating with are *human* and have these very same filters. Maybe your brother is tired of being pitched about your "next great invention"—the one that will *really* work this time—so the filter through which he will receive your message has diminished capacity. His assumptions about you, like them or not, exist. If you want to persuade or influence him, you are going to need to use a new filter. Maybe you need to be more enthusiastic than you've been in the past. Maybe you meet for lunch and present your idea in a pitch deck instead of over a beer while watching the game.

Speaking of delivery of your message, there's a persuasion philosophy you can almost always rely on—the Law of Indirect Effort. This law basically states that you have a better chance at getting what you want by *not directly* seeking it out from your prospect. Oftentimes, this means giving them something they need first, and then banking on earning their respect and reciprocation.

A great example of this is found in a YouTube clip about the popular Mark Wahlberg HBO hit *Entourage*.[46] In this compilation, we see a crusty Hollywood agent who has been in the business for decades and is trying to pitch a script based on the band,

---

46   Tubewoodycool. YouTube. June 07, 2010. Accessed October 02, 2021. https://www.youtube.com/watch?v=jBh0SpDoVZw.

The Ramones, to anyone who will listen. To do this, he repeats an iconic question in sales, "What if I told you [INSERT whatever it is you are giving to the prospect]? Would that interest you?" By the end of the clip, the Hollywood agent ends up asking the studio president, "What if I told you that you could make this movie for nothing, win an Oscar, and gross $100 million? Would that be something you'd be interested in?" To which the studio president says, "Yeah, that's something I'd be interested in." The trick here is that there is only one answer: yes. I mean, who wouldn't be interested in something beneficial that costs them nothing?

Boom. The Hollywood agent gets his first *yes* and the messaging momentum is building.

The ability to connect and persuade has everything to do with the messaging. Think about this analogy: are you a thermometer or a thermostat? A thermometer takes the temperature of the environment. But a thermostat actually takes the temperature *and* sets the conditions of the environment to make it hotter or colder.

Remember, *you* control the H2H selling environment. Now that you know how to set the conditions, let's start turning up the heat!

• •

H2H Reflections

- You only have 7 seconds to get your potential buyer's attention; don't make it about you!

- What do you usually say in the first 7 seconds with someone you want to persuade? Getting their attention is one thing. Keeping it is another. Do you frequently find yourself losing their attention within the next 21 seconds? Or maybe you make it to 63 seconds, then get your ask kicked.

- When trying to persuade someone, make sure to constantly check that your listening level is tracking toward empathy and sincerity.
- No matter how great your message, if it's not delivered properly, you'll never get your desired results. Check your leadership style: Tells, Sells, Consults, and Joins. Read-Offense: choose the right style for the right situation.
- Apply the right filter at the right time to the right situation.

• •

CHAPTER NINE:

The Language of Persuasion

• • •

"The difference between the almost right word and the right word is the difference between the lightning bug and the lightning."
- Mark Twain

Have you ever thought about what influences the amount you tip at a restaurant? Well, your server likely has. Sure, they are providing a service. After all, they rely on tips to make ends meet. In case you didn't know, the word *tips* is actually an acronym that means: To Insure Proper Service.

Servers use a variety of tactics to increase their tips. Some might comp dessert with a wink and a smile. Others draw a little smiley face on the paper bill. Some are very attentive and friendly, while others give you space to make sure they are not annoying but continue to watch from a distance. The thing is, very few of these tactics have been studied. Until 2005. It turns out, one simple action in particular can have an astronomical effect on the size of the tip you leave.

A study of tipping behavior in the Netherlands done by researcher, Rick van Baaren, found that mimicry improved tips—a phenomenon known as *The Parrot Effect.*[47] It goes like this:

You sit down at a restaurant, peruse the menu, then say to your server, "I'd like a burger with extra onions, no mustard, seasoned fries, and a pickle spear on the side with a Pepsi." When the server replies by repeating your order word for word, they increase the chances of a larger tip by 70 percent. Just by mimicking exactly the words you said—what we call using the buyer's language, also known as the language of persuasion.

But what are the components of the language of persuasion?

Verbal vs Nonverbal

Albert Mehrabian, Professor Emeritus of Psychology at the University of California, Los Angeles, asked those very same questions to understand the relative impact of both verbal and nonverbal communication.

In his book, *Silent Messages*, Mehrabian examines the important aspects of communication:[48]

1. Nonverbal Messages: What are the important nonverbal messages for effective persuasion of others, for example, in a supervisory role or in sales?

---

47   Baaren, Rick B. van. "The Parrot Effect: How to Increase Tip Size." Cornell Hotel and Restaurant Administration Quarterly 46, no. 1. 79–84. February 2005. https://doi.org/10.1177/0010880404270062.

48   Mehrabian, A. Silent messages: Implicit communication of emotions and attitudes. 1981. Belmont, CA: Wadsworth.

2. Deceitful Behavior: How can one detect that another is being deceitful or not overly forthcoming?

3. Individual Communication Styles: How do we describe a person's general communication style, and what are the basic elements of a person's style? How can one identify problem elements in one's own nonverbal communication and improve one's communication effectiveness?

4. Word Syntax: For example, what differences in attitudes are implied when someone says, "I like those people" instead of, "I like these people?"

5. Incongruent Communications: The relative importance of verbal and nonverbal messages.

When talking about the language of persuasion, we're talking about a combination of body language (including facial expressions), voice tone and word intonation, volume and speed of speech, and sentence syntax—the arrangement of the words in the sentence.

Mehrabian's study revealed something quite amazing: a formula known as the 7%-38%-55% Rule. These percentages relate to relative impact of verbal messaging, visual messaging, and vocal (tonal) messaging when persuading.

EFFECTIVENESS OF THE MESSAGE

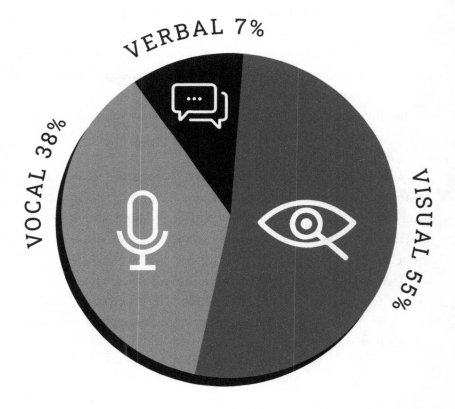

This breakdown is based on two studies done by Albert Mehrabian and his colleagues.[49]

---

49   Mehrabian, A. Silent messages: Implicit communication of emotions and attitudes. 1981.

Study #1

This first study involved having subjects listening to nine recorded words. Three of the words corresponded to liking (honey, dear, and thanks), three corresponded with neutrality (maybe, really, and oh) and three expressed dislike (don't, brute, and terrible).

These sets of words were spoken in various tones, then the subjects had to guess the emotions behind the words. Mehrabian found that tone carried more meaning than the words themselves.

Study #2

This time around, the subjects were asked to listen to a recording of a female saying a single word (maybe) in three different tones to cover the emotion of (1) liking something or someone, (2) neutrality, and (3) disliking something or someone.

Next, the subjects were shown photos of female faces with the same three emotions and were asked to guess the emotions in the recorded voices, the photos, and both in combination. The photos got more accurate responses than the voice by a ratio of three to two.

So, what did the data show? When using the language of persuasion:

- 7% of your impact is through your words
- 38% of your impact happens through the tone of your voice
- 55% of your impact happens through visual input

But remember that these statistics are only relevant when the message is *incongruent*—when the words, body language, and tone do not line up. This means that understanding tone and body language are critical to being able to connect and persuade. You may have guessed this to be true about body language, but think for a moment about the importance of tone. Consider the following sentence:

She isn't flying to Paris tomorrow.

Simple enough, right? But how did *you* read it? Based on which word the emphasis is on, you receive a totally different message. Here is what I mean:

She isn't flying to Paris tomorrow.

With the emphasis on *she*, the communicator is implying that your assumption about who exactly is flying to Paris is wrong.

She isn't ***flying*** to Paris tomorrow.

In this instance, we're being led to believe that perhaps she is making the trip to Paris, but she isn't *flying* at all but possibly taking another form of transportation.

She isn't flying to ***Paris*** tomorrow.

With the emphasis on *Paris*, clearly, the capital of France isn't even in the equation. She is obviously flying somewhere, but it's not Paris.

She isn't flying to Paris ***tomorrow***.

In this case, she's flying alright. And she's Paris-bound. It may be next week or next year, but it is definitely not *tomorrow*.

Intonation and emphasis in your words is *everything* when trying to connect and persuade (see what I did there?). This means we need to be very careful with words-only communications, such as emails and texts. It's very easy to misunderstand the meaning behind the message, even if you are using emoticons. This also means that you can get someone to pay more attention to your body language by intentionally being less clear with your words. If you want them to trust the words, be clear and unambiguous.

But how can you use body language effectively? Isn't that something natural and intuitive that we can't control? Not necessarily. Read on.

Saying It Without Words

When you are talking with someone and they cross their arms, roll their eyes, or check their phone, you will likely think that they are drifting or closing themselves off from the conversation. But how many other nonverbal cues are you actually missing? And are you really interpreting those body language expressions correctly? What if they are waiting to hear back from a loved one in the hospital? What if they check their watch to make sure they have enough time to chat with you because they are moved by what you are saying. Out of context and when judging isolated movements, body language can be easy to misinterpret.

But there is a right way to use body language in communication. Here is a rundown of how to use and read body language to effectively persuade and influence—the 3 C's of Nonverbal Communication:[50]

---

50 Thompson, J. Semiotics & nonverbal communication [Web log post]. 2012, March 23. Retrieved from http://semionaut.net/semiotics-nonverbal-communication-3/

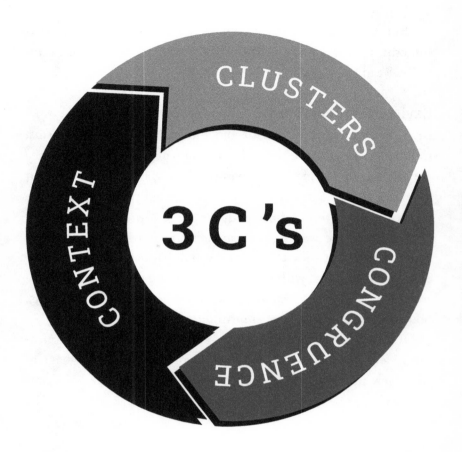

Clusters

Never judge somebody on a single body movement. Instead, look for clusters of movements that add up to an accurate conclusion. For example, if the other person crosses their arms, leans backwards, and also frowns, you are getting clear signals of disagreement. If an individual is not making eye contact *and* fidgeting with jewelry or other items, it may be a sign that they are uncomfortable or not engaged. However, if they simply don't make eye contact but are taking notes, it may not be a sign of being uncomfortable or disagreement.

Congruence

The words spoken must be taken into context of the nonverbal cues. For an accurate interpretation of how someone is receiving your message, their words, tone, and body language need to be aligned, that is, *congruent*. For example, if you ask someone if they are okay, and they respond, "I'm fine," but it's obvious from slumped shoulders or other body language that something is wrong, this would be non-congruence.

Context

When analyzing your audience, consider not only their nonverbal cues, but also the environment in which the interaction is taking place...as well as the history between the people communicating. The immediate environment can have a clear effect—for example, when people are around others they find attractive, they might do a little preening, a little more laughing, and a lot more talking than usual. The wider context of a person's life also has an effect on their body language, indicating things like anxiety or excitement. When trying to connect with someone, look at their baseline behaviors—is the person an introvert or extrovert? Because the body language of the introvert will be much more subtle. The person's general mood is something else to consider when evaluating body language. A sad person, for example, may not exhibit very obvious signals, so you need to watch closely.

The thing is, communication requires at least two people. This means there is an invisible tennis match of signals going back and forth that each person responds to. When someone shifts position, rubs their eyes, or checks their watch they are sending cues to how they are receiving the message. When communicating, always watch for transitions in which their body language changes. Maybe they cross their arms. Maybe they sit down. This could indicate the conversation has gone on too long and they are just being polite. When you see a change in body language, think backward to any cues that may have triggered the transition. Maybe they start to lean in, which means they are investing more into the conversation.

So now that we understand more about body language, what are some things you can do to impact your power of persuasion with body language? Here are some tips from ChangingMinds.org:[51]

Open Assertion

Make sure your posture is open and welcoming as you are inviting them in and ready to listen. Open body language involves movement that is relaxed and deliberate. It should mirror what you are saying and not have any unnecessary movements (swaying, tapping, etc.) that could reveal anxiety or uncomfortableness.

Match and Move

Just like with the *Parrot Effect*, make sure to begin by reflecting their movements back to them, matching their body language to create an emotional bond . Keep your body at the same height whenever possible. Then comes the magic. Once your body movements are aligned, start moving differently. If they have bonded with you, they will now be following *you* rather than you following them. If they're not in sync with you, keep matching and moving until they are. Do not move to the close until they are following you.

---

51   Sales Body Language. Accessed October 02, 2021. http://changingminds.org/disciplines/sales/articles/sales_body_language.html.

Lean In

When you lean in toward someone, you are literally getting closer to them, which creates an H2H bond. The only caveat is that the person may see you as trying to invade their personal space if you try this tactic too soon. But if that bond has been created, when coupled with lowering your voice to a whisper, leaning in can set the stage for the person to feel like they are hearing exclusive information, which our human brain can't resist. Leaning in is also a move that allows you to get close to someone without expressing dominance.

Subtle Moves

Sometimes the most power-packed persuasion moves are the most subtle. Here are some examples:

- Raising your eyebrows or tilting your head slightly to show questioning or surprise.
- Pausing and holding your breath after asking a question.
- Pressing lips slightly together to show disagreement.
- Gently smiling to show agreement and comfort with the situation.
- Slow and deep breathing with relaxed face to show confidence.
- Slightly wince when they mention things that are outside your intent.
- Gesture with open palms to show openness.
- Regular soft eye contact that shows caring as opposed to staring at them.

The most important thing to remember is to be acutely aware of dominant body language or power moves. I've seen too many salespeople try to take the position of control and derail all their efforts. Nobody wants to feel like they are being pressured or controlled.

Showing you have authority over a particular subject is necessary to convince the person that you are worth listening to. But don't be a know-it-all. And make sure your body language matches what you say, otherwise people will perceive that you are lying. The most effective way to accomplish this is to manage your thoughts, which will naturally shape your body language.

Show respect for the person you hope to connect with and persuade…but also show respect for yourself. Whoever it is, remember that you are equal to them—no better and no worse.

Now that you have the tone and body language down, let's get to saying what needs to be said.

The Science of Storytelling

When you're trying to persuade someone, there are a finite number of ways you can engage them. You can open with trying to teach them something using data and information. You can share something personal to build trust. Or you can ask a question to get them thinking. But whatever your approach is, you better lean on the science of storytelling to deliver your message.

In a recent study, the following two paragraphs were presented to subjects to see which one generated more donations:[52]

A) Any money that you donate will go to Rokia, a seven-year-old girl who lives in Mali in Africa. Rokia is desperately poor and faces a threat of severe hunger, even starvation. Her life will be

---

52 "To Increase Charitable Donations Appeal to the Heart not the Head". Knowledge@Wharton. Jun 27, 2007. Accessed October 02, 2021. https://knowledge.wharton.upenn.edu/article/to-increase-charitable-donations-appeal-to-the-heart-not-the-head/

changed for the better as a result of your financial gift. With your support, and the support of other caring sponsors, Save the Children will work with Rokia's family and other members of the community to help feed and educate her, and provide her with basic medical care.

B) Food shortages in Malawi are affecting more than three million children. In Zambia, severe rainfall deficits have resulted in a 42% drop in maize production from 2000. As a result, an estimated three million Zambians face hunger. Four million Angolans — one-third of the population — have been forced to flee their homes. More than 11 million people in Ethiopia need immediate food assistance.

Which description do you think received more contributions from people? If you answered A, you are correct. According to the study conducted by Deborah Small, a Wharton marketing professor, the research showed that if organizations want to raise money for a cause, it is far better to appeal to the heart than to the head.[53] Put another way, feelings, not analytical thinking, drive donations.

The fact is, people forget facts, but they remember stories. The data in this study actually showed that we are hardwired to intake and remember stories differently than any other mode of information. The research also showed that stories are two times more persuasive than raw data.

Aristotle was onto the science of storytelling 2000 years ago when he said that metaphors are what give a language its *verbal beauty*. "To be a master of metaphor is the greatest thing by far," he once wrote.[54] Metaphors instantly convey feelings, logic, value,

---

53 "To Increase Charitable Donations Appeal to the Heart not the Head". Knowledge@Wharton. Jun 27, 2007.
54 Aristotle, and Freese, John Henry. *The "art" of Rhetoric*. Cambridge, MA: Harvard Univ. Press, 2000.

and wisdom to those you want to persuade and influence. It gives the intangible and abstract real meaning. *Forbes* writer, Carmine Gallo, wrote that billionaire Warren Buffett "is frequently asked why 90 percent of his investments are made in the U.S. He answers in metaphor: 'America's economic soil remains fertile.' Buffett's explanation could fill books, but in five words a metaphor allows him to communicate complexity, simply. And that's the beauty of metaphor."[55]

If you want to master the art of persuasion, master the metaphor. But as Aristotle also said, keep it brief. In this fast-paced world of sound bites, tweets, and five-second ads, brevity is a critical skill in the Human Sales Factor. "Aristotle had discovered that there are fairly universal limits to the amount of information which any human can absorb and retain," wrote Kings College professor Edith Hall in her book, *Aristotle's Way*. "When it comes to persuasion, less is always more."[56]

> **If you want to master the art of persuasion, master the metaphor.**

Aristotle also said that the opening of any presentation is where the power is.[57] Never save your best points for the big reveal at the end. Start strong and you will finish strong.

55   Gallo, Carmine. "Warren Buffett Loves This Ancient Tool Of Persuasion To Enliven His Annual Letters." Forbes. February 25, 2018. Accessed October 02, 2021. https://www.forbes.com/sites/carminegallo/2018/02/25/warren-buffett-loves-this-ancient-tool-of-persuasion-to-enliven-his-annual-letters/?sh=a1952277fda7.
56   Hall, Edith. *Aristotle's Way: How Ancient Wisdom Can Change Your Life*. 2019.
57   Aristotle, and Freese, John Henry. *The "art" of Rhetoric*. 2000.

Rules of Engagement

Remember the opening pitch of the guy in the *Shark Tank* example earlier in the book? He was actually pretty lucky to have recovered. Because according to the data, once the opening of a pitch is botched by being unprepared or ineffective, the ability to connect and persuade is quickly lost.

The *Wall Street Journal* conducted a Motivational Systems survey of twenty-two large company Vice Presidents about the effectiveness of presentations.[58] They concluded:

- Only 3 percent of the presentations were found stimulating by the VPs.
- 40 percent made the VPs sleepy.
- 44 percent were straight-up boring.
- 13 percent fell into other categories reflecting that the presentations were not useful.

---

58   Motivational Systems survey of 200 large company VPs. *Wall Street Journal.* Accessed October 2, 2021. https://maximizevalue.com/5-ways-to-improve-your-next-sales-presentation/

The Challenge: ENGAGEMENT

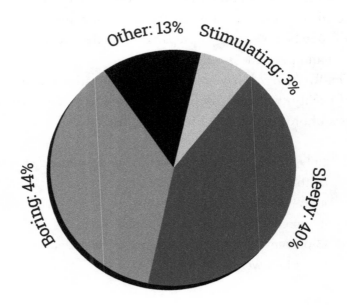

Whether you are trying to influence one person or one hundred, the challenge with persuasion is how to be engaging and stimulating.

One way to be engaging and stimulating in the opening is by asking something known as a QBOT, which stands for a Question Bearing On Time. This will swing the attention to the time blocked on the person's calendar. By invoking the universal concept of time, you are showing that you value their most prized asset. You might say, "How much time is too much today?" or, "Does the fifteen minutes you blocked off for our meeting still work for you?" Asking a QBOT gives you the high ground. You are in control, but you're allowing *them* to feel in control by getting a say-so in how much time they're willing to spend with you.

Once you have their buy-in pertaining to time, you need to clearly state the objective or the purpose of the meeting. The key here is to remember that the Human Sales Factor is all about the buyer. You need to state the objective or purpose in *their* terms by saying something like, "Our meeting today will give you options or ideas to consider." *Our meeting* is possessive plural, so they feel that they are getting something out of the meeting. By stating the objective, you are answering for them why you are speaking. It also creates value for them to spend their time as well as understand

> **A Why Speak Statement not only gives the person a roadmap, but it also gives you one as well.**

your intent. This is showing them the destination on the map. Now, it's time to give them an idea of how to get there.

Do this by rolling out a brief agenda. It should be laid out in the same order that the buyer thinks or prioritizes. Typically, when you are engaging, they're thinking, "So what does this person want? How's this relevant to me? How can we partner together? What could be some next steps?" Your dialogue might sound something like, "I'll ask you some questions, determine if this is an option for you, see if there's a fit, and we'll take next steps."

Now you are on your way to creating an environment where they understand why you're asking certain questions. With that understanding, they might be more candid or willing to answer because they know where you're driving them and what's in it for them at the end of the road.

A key to making this an effective tactic is making what we call a *Why Speak Statement*. A Why Speak Statement not only gives the person a roadmap, but it also gives you one as well. That boosts your confidence. It should only take about 20 seconds if it's done well, and it gives you control of your meeting. At the end, add, "Is there anything you want to add or change? How does that sound?" Asking these types of questions allows you to set the agenda but also allows them to feel involved in what you are about to discuss during your meeting together. It's another high-ground move.

When in the meeting and using questions to understand their needs, it shouldn't be "more equals better." In fact, sometimes that can come across as interrogative. It's actually more about how you facilitate a two-way dialogue. This is where having control and setting expectations early in the meeting helps to better guide the conversation.

Identify your true objective of the meeting. Develop questions that are going to be impactful based on that objective. What information do you need to find out? What are the knowledge gaps? Planning all this ahead of time takes the pressure off of you in the moment so that you can be agile with your EQ and adaptable to the person you're engaging. It also provides more structure to the conversation.

Increasing awareness of EQ, reading people in situations, and taking the time to prepare allows you to be more confident as you connect with the buyer H2H. The more engagements that are structured this way, the more the Human Sales Factor can be mastered.

But sometimes...

When the Going Gets Tough

Sometimes the information you want to present is difficult. Sometimes the person you want to connect with and persuade is being difficult. And sometimes the environment itself is presenting challenges that are frustrating and throwing off your mojo. Have you ever been in the middle of a very important conversation, just about to the punchline, when suddenly your phone rings? Or an ambulance screams past? Or the server interrupts asking if a warm-up on coffee is needed?

Well, the Human Sales Factor provides some tactics for handling difficult situations in the moment:

- Maintain a positive attitude in pressure situations.
- Be flexible and respond positively to fluid situations.
- Compose yourself when in uncomfortable situations or fielding difficult questions.
- Communicate clearly when under pressure.
- Sell yourself *and* your message while in pressure situations.
- Anticipate questions.
- Prepare positive messages.
- Prepare anecdotes, personal experiences, and other supporting evidence.
- Pay special attention to your appearance and body language.
- Make sure your hands are comfortable.
- Make eye contact.
- Respond thoughtfully and promptly.
- Avoid appearing unprepared.

As Hemingway said: "Courage is grace under pressure."[59] In difficult situations, be graceful as hell.

You have to get past the notion that motivation is something one person does to another. Motivation, by its very definition, comes from *within*. You simply need to set the right conditions for someone to move toward your idea on their own.

---

59   Hemingway, Ernest. *New Yorker*. Interview. 1929. Accessed October 2, 2021. https://jfk.blogs.archives.gov/2018/07/20/jfk-hemingway/

Three key questions you need to consider when you approach someone you hope to motivate is:

- What do you want them to *feel*?
- What do you want them to *know*?
- What do you want them to *do*?

With these questions as your guide, you can consistently move toward closing the deal with whomever you want about anything you want any time you want.

And when, finally, you become the thermostat and not just the thermometer, *you* are the guru on the hill, making them look in the mirror.

. . . .

H2H Reflections

- Become fluent in the language of persuasion—the buyer's language!
- Be sure to have congruence in you body language (including facial expressions), voice tone and word intonation, volume and speed of speech, and sentence syntax—the arrangement of the words in you sentences.
- Look for clusters of verbal and nonverbal communication in your buyer. Beware of jumping to conclusions!
- When speaking with your prospective buyer, be open, match and move, lean in, and use subtle moves to persuade and influence.
- People forget facts, but they remember stories. Master the metaphor!
- Be engaging and stimulating by asking a QBOT—a Question Bearing On Time.

. . . .

CONCLUSION:

It All Comes Down to You

• • •

"Every new beginning comes from some other beginning's end."
- Seneca

When you think about persuasion and influence, remember that this is a game that's been going on for thousands of years. Humans trying to persuade other humans to join a cause, or sack a city, or build an empire, or migrate out of one continent to another. Whatever your goal is, you first need to look in the mirror and zero in on your personal reasons *why*.

Like Dr. Seuss said in the poem Oh, The Places You'll Go!, "I'm afraid that sometimes you'll play lonely games too. Games you can't win 'cause you'll play against you."60 You can be your own worst enemy sometimes. Or your best friend. When you look in the mirror, you get to decide if what you're trying to influence

---

60   Geisel, Theodor. *Oh, The Places You'll Go!* New York: Random House. 1960.

someone to do or persuade someone to think is worth it. Do you have the enthusiasm to sell whatever it is you are selling? Are you bought into the idea yourself?

The Human Sales Factor is your ability to connect human-to-human. But remember, we are not creatures of logic, we're creatures of emotion. Once you deal with your own emotions, only then can you deal with the emotions of other people. And sometimes the rational argument doesn't always win. Appealing to and understanding people's emotions is not a one size fits most. Sometimes those motivations to do something might not be exactly aligned with what you want. That's why you need to see the world through your prospective buyer's eyes.

Then, as you gaze out the metaphoric window and attempt to reach through, you need to understand the *how* behind making that connection with people. How you present yourself, how you listen, how you deliver your message. These are all concepts that deserve a deeper dive than covered in these pages. Especially those concerning leadership. But that's for another book.

As Leonardo DaVinci said, "Art is never finished, only abandoned."

ABOUT THE AUTHOR

Lance Tyson is an American businessman, bestselling author, sales consultant, and President and CEO of Tyson Group, which provide sales training and coaching for world-renown brands like the Dallas Cowboys, San Francisco 49ers, Fenway Sports Management, Boston Red Sox, Legends, Madison Square Garden, and Eli Lilly. Tyson is known for his sales presentations and unique methodology, demonstrated in his first book, *Selling is an Away Game: Close Business and Compete in a Complex World* (published in 2018).

Lance Tyson was born in Norristown, Pennsylvania and attended Pottsgrove High School, from which he graduated in 1988. Tyson went on to study at Penn State University and Thomas Edison State College in New Jersey, where he received a degree in History.

An industry leader in sales training, development, and management, Lance Tyson is passionate about sharing his knowledge with others to help them achieve sales success in today's erratic, ever-changing marketplace. He has led countless workshops, trainings, and keynote presentations for audiences of all sizes. With decades of experience in his field, Lance can present with authority on any topic in the realm of sales and leadership.

For more from Lance Tyson, or if you are ready to supercharge your sales team, please visit TysonGroup.com.

A free ebook edition is available with the purchase of this book.

To claim your free ebook edition:

1. Visit MorganJamesBOGO.com
2. Sign your name CLEARLY in the space
3. Complete the form and submit a photo of the entire copyright page
4. You or your friend can download the ebook to your preferred device

Morgan James
BOGO™

A **FREE** ebook edition is available for you or a friend with the purchase of this print book.

CLEARLY SIGN YOUR NAME ABOVE

Instructions to claim your free ebook edition:
1. Visit MorganJamesBOGO.com
2. Sign your name CLEARLY in the space above
3. Complete the form and submit a photo of this entire page
4. You or your friend can download the ebook to your preferred device

Print & Digital Together Forever.

Snap a photo

Free ebook

Read anywhere